discover Joy in your Marriage

discover Joy in your Marriage

Living the Beatitudes

Adam and Joy Bodzioch

DPI
DISCIPLESHIP
PUBLICATIONS
INTERNATIONAL

www.dpibooks.org

Discover Joy in Your Marriage
©2012 by DPI Books
5016 Spedale Court #331
Spring Hill, TN 37174

Printed in the United States of America

Cover Design: Brian Branch
Interior Design: Thais Gloor

ISBN: 978-1-57782-334-6

Contents

How to Most Effectively Use This Book

Discover Joy in Your Marriage will use Bible-teaching, real-life vignettes and forty-three practical exercises to help you cooperate with God in creating a marriage that goes beyond your dreams or expectations.

Here is some helpful information to help you get the most out of the book.

The chapters take you through a series of steps for growing in love and intimacy by including, at the end of each major point, exercises and discussion questions for you and your spouse to complete together or in a small group setting.

Arrange for both you and your spouse to read and complete the exercises at the same time with the goal of being ready to discuss your answers immediately afterward.

Although there are some separate exercises for husbands and wives, we recommend that each of you have your own copy of the book so you can be reading and completing the exercises in parallel fashion.

You will need a separate dedicated notebook to respond to the exercises. They are numbered to help you keep up with where you are in your responses.

Used in this way, we believe this book will allow God to transform your marriage into a light that illuminates the way, guiding others to the kind of family life he intends.

Introduction

For many years, I (Joy) believed that God wanted me to fully experience his joy, but try as I might, I always felt controlled by my circumstances: I felt good in the good times, but discouraged, fearful or anxious in the difficult times. As a psychologist I wanted to find the "keys" to joy for myself, but also for my clients.

Finally, one day in 2004 while reading Jesus' Sermon on the Mount, God suddenly revealed his secrets for joy and "vibrant mental health." The more I studied the Beatitudes, the more convinced I became that this passage is God's "Royal Road" for finding that fulfillment Jesus came to bring us! Of course I wanted to share this news with everyone, so I wrote *Discover Joy: Well-Being God's Way.*[1]

God passionately longs to bless you with a life of fulfillment and joy. Your part is to wholeheartedly travel the path laid out in Matthew 5:3–12. *Discover Joy* is a guide for that personal journey.

Now, several years later, Adam and I are excited to offer this sequel since Christ's Beatitudes can also lead you to *Discover Joy in Your Marriage!*

1

As Christ Loved the Church

Let her love alone fill you with delight.
Proverbs 5:19b TLB

We met in 1964 and married in 1966—a very long time ago! And although we've been married many years and have written this workbook, we haven't arrived or learned everything about having an amazing marriage.

Our relationship began with some high hopes (born mostly of '50s TV shows such as *Leave It to Beaver* and *The Donna Reed Show*), but also some strong doubts (from observing the reality of our parents' marriages). We've had some wonderful times together. But throughout the years we also survived worldly attitudes, destructive habits, pride, deceit, selfishness, adultery and other sins too numerous to list here.

Our marriage had begun to improve in the early '90s thanks to a Marriage Encounter weekend we attended, but the real work (and transformation) began when we both studied the Bible and were baptized into Christ. We not only received a new Spirit, but also a growing vision for the kind of marriage God intends.

We are incredibly grateful to the couples who have counseled us. Thanks to their friendship, patience and gentle care, our marriage continues to grow and thrive even as we keep learning.

We have also been honored to touch the lives of many couples who trusted us with their deepest feelings and vulnerabilities. Thank you for inviting us into your lives to work with God.

Finally, we express our gratitude to the staff of the Mexico City Church of Christ, who graciously invited us to conduct a workshop for their marriage ministry based on this material. What a blessing it has been to help restore broken relationships and rekindle the love that once burned so brightly! This workbook is a culmination of these experiences, so we dedicate it to all those couples who opened and shared their lives with us. Helping each other is always a mutual blessing!

Developing a Vision

> He made each. He made them to fit together as two halves of a perfect whole. Only He knows the secret of love by which two can be made one. It is only through Him that the human heart ever knows love. He draws out to Himself the love of each, to the full, as no human being ever can. He puts into each the great tender passion for the other, and the yet greater, and yet more tender passion for Himself.[1]

These beautiful words express what we all want for our marriages: to be a "perfect whole" with "great tender passion" for each other. This is the stuff of romantic tales that melt our hearts. We are made in the image of our God who *is* love, and who envisions that we experience passionate love for another human as we build amazing, inspirational marriages. And he doesn't stop there. He "has given us everything we need for life and godliness" (2 Peter 1:3), enabling us to actually fulfill his vision! Biblically this is true. Why, then, does it contradict what we observe: countless couples in the church who live "lives of quiet desperation"[2]—hopeless about the possibility of change?

A headline in the April 4, 2008, *Christian Post E-Newsletter* read, "Christian Divorce Rate Identical to National Average." The article indicated that evangelical Christians have the same divorce rate as other married couples, with 35% having married and divorced at least once. According to researcher George Barna,

> There no longer seems to be much of a stigma attached to divorce; it is now seen as an unavoidable rite of passage. Interviews with young adults suggest that they want their initial marriage to last, but are not particularly optimistic about that possibility. There is also evidence that many young people are moving toward embracing the idea of serial marriage, in which a person gets married two or three times, seeking a different partner for each phase of their adult life.[3]

In the midst of this bad news about marriage, God wants to empower us to live victorious lives that satisfy our needs while inspiring and attracting our non-Christian neighbors.

Paul encouraged the Philippians with these words: "For God is working in you, giving you the desire and the power to do what pleases him" (NLT). Memorize this verse; it holds the key! Regardless of your interpersonal skills or Bible knowledge or hard work, you will never create an exciting, godly marriage on your own power. The only way to *Discover Joy in Your Marriage* is to daily crucify pride and selfishness, and to crown Jesus as Lord of your life and relationships. Fortunately, Jesus left us a step-by-step plan for doing just that!

Personalizing the Vision

Earlier we mentioned God's vision for marriage. Now let's begin to develop a vision for our marriages. Before we start, though, consider the question, "Do we even know what a healthy marriage looks like?" Most importantly, if research provides answers to this question, does the Bible agree with or expand that answer?

First, it's important to differentiate "health" from "dysfunction." As families go, what distinguishes the dysfunctional from the healthy, and what do marriages look like in these families? For over three decades, psychiatrist Robert Beavers and his widely respected team of researchers have worked to answer these questions. The outcome is an assessment instrument known as "The Beavers Scale of Family Health and Competence," which describes five levels of family health.[4]

It turns out that the cohesiveness of families is determined by the quality of the marriage relationship. In the healthiest families, everyone feels secure because parents form an effective coalition and are able to work as a team. In other words, the well-being of the adults and condition of the marriage will most strongly influence the ultimate health of the family unit.

Most importantly, the researchers say that the primary difference between "adequate" and "optimal" families is that in optimal families the spouses truly "delight in each other."

But what is God's expectation for marriage? God describes his love for Zion as "The City of God's Delight" and the "Bride of God." He says, "For the Lord delights in you and will claim you as his bride" (Isaiah 62:4 NLT). Notice how God describes his feeling for his bride as *delight*.

In the New Testament, Paul instructs husbands: "Love your wives just as Christ loved the church and gave himself up for her" (Ephesians 5:25). Since Jesus said, "As the Father has loved me, so have I loved you" (John 15:9), we also see that husbands are to love their wives in the same way God loves Jesus. Finally, referring to Jesus, Isaiah prophesies,

> "Here is my servant, whom I uphold,
>   my chosen one in whom I delight;
> I will put my Spirit on him
>   and he will bring justice to the nations." (Isaiah 42:1)

Coming full circle, we conclude that, since "delight" describes Christ's love for the church, it should also describe the relationship between a husband and wife.

As I reflected in *Discover Joy,* it's exciting and faith-building to discover that Scripture was accurately describing the characteristics of mental health 2000 years before psychology existed. In this case the research again agrees with Scripture: A healthy marriage is one in which husbands and wives delight in each other. This is the marriage that creates the strongest possible foundation for a healthy family. As we'll see, this is a marriage in which children thrive and learn to make Jesus Lord of their lives. And it's a marriage that pleases and glorifies God.

But what does it really mean to "delight in" our spouse? "Delight in" is defined as "take pleasure from" and synonyms include "admire, adore, appreciate, be content, be pleased, cherish, enjoy, love, luxuriate in, relish and savor." (Ask yourself: Is this the way I feel about my spouse?) Here are a few signs of marital delight:

- Touching each other frequently (even after many years of marriage)
- Having fun doing mundane activities such as grocery shopping, chatting over dinner, painting a room, walking in the neighborhood or sitting on the porch

- Experiencing as much pleasure together during quiet evenings at home as when surrounded by friends
- Sharing many common interests
- Finding joy sharing simple things: a fire on a cold night, a rainbow, cuddling on the sofa, reading the newspaper
- Sharing stimulating conversation
- Enjoying a "best friendship" that grows through the challenging times as well as the good times
- Being eager to confide in each other quickly and first
- Trusting the other to be gentle during disagreements and when we are not at our best

I know that as some of you read the characteristics of a "delightful" marriage above, your heart sinks. You think, "I can't even begin to imagine having a marriage like this." If those are your thoughts, please don't give up. Read on. As all journeys begin with the first step, so does this one. Even if your marriage seems dead right now, please decide to believe one more time in the regenerative power of our God. Just do your best, and look for and celebrate even small signs of growth.

Living the Beatitudes in Your Marriage

Finally, how do we know that the Beatitudes are a reliable guide for helping us learn to delight in each other? *Discover Joy* was based on the idea that living the Beatitudes results in a consistent experience of joy, regardless of our outward circumstances. And since the Beatitudes are both personal *and interpersonal,* they can also bring joy to our relationships. In fact, the Amplified version renders Matthew 5:3–5 as follows:

> Blessed (happy, to be envied, and spiritually prosperous with life-joy and satisfaction in God's favor and salvation, regardless of their outward conditions) are the poor in spirit (the humble, who rate themselves insignificant), for theirs is the kingdom of heaven!

> Blessed and enviably happy [with a happiness produced by the experience of God's favor and especially conditioned by the revelation of His matchless grace] are those who mourn, for they shall be comforted!

> Blessed (happy, blithesome, joyous, spiritually prosperous with life-joy and satisfaction in God's favor and salvation, regardless of their outward conditions) are the meek (the mild, patient, long-suffering) for they shall inherit the earth!

These descriptions certainly *sound* like delight to us!

Couples often ask for our help because they know Joy is a psychologist. Then they're surprised (and sometimes disappointed) to discover that almost all of what we teach comes from the Bible!

After counseling with couples inside and outside the church, we have never been more convinced that only the Bible reveals the secrets for building extraordinary marriages that are satisfying, inspiring and Christ honoring. We also believe that the Beatitudes are intended, not just as a "Royal Road" to personal blessing, vibrant mental health and joy, but also as a step-by-step guide for growing more in love with God *and each other!*

Are you ready to begin? If so, the first step is to...*decide to trust God's way!*

2

Decide to Trust God's Way

"Blessed are the poor in spirit,
for theirs is the kingdom of heaven."
Matthew 5:3

At the time of our wedding we considered ourselves "good people." We had both grown up in church-going families. We were law-abiding people who believed in old-fashioned values such as honesty, integrity, loyalty and fairness. We were both self-reliant, believing the (unbiblical) folk wisdom that "God helps those who help themselves."

It never occurred to us that we did not have the innate ability to build a good marriage. In fact, we didn't even think of marriage that way. We figured that the old Beatles' song was true: "All You Need Is Love." Once we tied the knot, we thought a great relationship would automatically happen. And when it looked like things weren't turning out as we'd hoped, we had no clue about how to make it better.

Our marriage only began to improve when we faced the fact that we did *not* have the personal qualities or tools to build a great—or even good—marriage. In '79 Joy had begun work on her graduate degree in psychology, and one of her first classes was Marital & Family Therapy. This was an eye-opener for both of us as she shared what she was learning.

Then, following a Marriage Encounter weekend, we began to realize that after sixteen years of marriage, we didn't even *know each other*. Although it would be many more years before we both became true disciples of Jesus, God was working at humbling our hearts.

Psalm 25:9 teaches that "he guides the humble in what is right and teaches them his way." Humility is always the first step to an improved relationship. Growing in our marriages first requires recognizing that we don't know what we're doing so we need God's help! This lays the groundwork for all the other steps.

Jesus is clear in the first beatitude: All of us must face that we are bankrupt, destitute and lacking the ability to do anything truly worthwhile on our own power. This is the essence of spiritual poverty: We do not have the attitude or aptitude for building a great life or a great marriage. Then we will acknowledge our continual need for grace and *decide to trust God's way*.

Go for Great!

Do we even know what we're missing? In marriages where there is frequent open hostility and arguing, it is no secret that something is wrong. These warring couples know they need help, although they may not know what kind of marriage they want. But when partners don't fight, this can create an illusion of marital unity and satisfaction. And, as marriage and family therapists discover, this appearance rarely represents reality!

One problem is that even though we might have a few models for successful marriage, we are not really sure what "God's way" for marriage looks like. Since the media provides many examples of horrifying non-Christian marriage, modern couples may opt for a relationship that is *at least* better than what they see on TV. They settle for "peace, peace...when there is no peace" (Jeremiah 8:11) rather than go for the great marriages God destined for them.

On the other hand, we have never worked with a husband and wife who both enjoyed a strong relationship with God, but whose marriage was in serious trouble. Building a deeper, more consistent walk with God is guaranteed to have a positive impact on our relationships, especially with our spouse and family members. Since love is a fruit of God's Spirit, when we grow closer to God, we become more loving to people. This is because he is working within and through us, making us more like Jesus. Little by little, we begin to demonstrate the qualities listed in 1 Corinthians 13:4–7:

> Love is patient, love is kind. It does not envy, it does not boast, it is not proud. It is not rude, it is not self-seeking, it is not easily angered, it keeps no record of wrongs. Love does not delight in evil but rejoices with the truth. It always protects, always trusts, always hopes, always perseveres. Love never fails. (1 Corinthians 13:4–8)

The fact that Jesus began the *first words* of the *first sermon* in the *first book* of the New Testament with a discourse about how we can be blessed suggests that God passionately *wants* to bless us! And since biblical marriage is intended to last throughout our adult years, isn't it reasonable that God designed it as our primary source of enrichment and blessing? We must trust God in this and choose to pursue his way, even if it's difficult to imagine the kind of intimacy and joy that could be ours.

Marriage, God's Way: What Does It Look Like?

What is God's idea of "a perfect marriage"? Unfortunately, we have only one very brief glimpse of marriage without sin:

> Now the Lord God said, It is not good (sufficient, satisfactory) that the man should be alone; I will make him a helper meet (suitable, adapted, complementary) for him. And out of the ground the Lord God formed every [wild] beast and living creature of the field and every bird of the air and brought them to Adam to see what he would call them; and whatever Adam called every living creature, that was its name.
>
> And Adam gave names to all the livestock and to the birds of the air and to every [wild] beast of the field; but for Adam there was not found a helper meet (suitable, adapted, complementary) for him. And the Lord God caused a deep sleep to fall upon Adam; and while he slept, He took one of his ribs or a part of his side and closed up the [place with] flesh. And the rib or part of his side which the Lord God had taken from the man He built up and made into a woman, and He brought her to the man.
>
> Then Adam said, This [creature] is now bone of my bones and flesh of my flesh; she shall be called Woman, because she was taken out of a man. Therefore a man shall leave his father and his mother and shall become united and cleave to his wife, and they shall become one flesh. And the man and his wife were both naked and were not embarrassed or ashamed in each other's presence. (Genesis 2:18–25 Amp)

In this passage we see that

- God created woman from man so spouses could *complement* and help each other.
- Marriage involves "leaving and cleaving"—leaving parents and replacing this bond with a new emotional and physical union.

- God expects us to be completely naked (exposed) to each other, both physically and emotionally, and to be *comfortable* with this kind of openness.

Taking a closer look at each of these bullets and applying them to our own marriages can help us decide whether our marriages reflect the first beatitude and living God's way.

#1 – Complementary Traits: Learning to Help and Complete Each Other

The word "complement" is sometimes confused with "compliment." Although it's certainly great to compliment (praise) your spouse, to complement your spouse means something else. It is to *complete* him or her. That Eve was taken from Adam's side is a beautiful illustration of this. God intends us to "round out" our spouse because each of us is *incomplete* without the other. Together we form a unified whole, enhancing our spouse, and balancing and strengthening the relationship.

Does this mean that "opposites attract?" In some ways. The truth is that people are usually attracted to others with similar likes and dislikes. But when it comes to choosing a marriage partner, in fact, we do look for someone whose personality characteristics complement (complete) ours, which then increases our ability to learn, heal and grow together over a lifetime. (Once again modern science confirms that the Bible has been presenting the best way all along.)

The problem occurs, of course, when we fight the differences rather than respect and appreciate them as sources of potential strength for the relationship.

Speaking from personal experience, we have very different ways of thinking and making decisions. We entered marriage with no awareness of these differences, and as a result, we often thought the other person was being unreasonable or unloving. No matter how much we discussed some issues, it seemed we still weren't able to come to an agreement. That, coupled with poor communication skills, made joint problem-solving like walking through a mine field!

One of us would eventually give in, which didn't *feel* right but seemed to be the only way to move forward. Since we never really resolved things, all those negative feelings just got swept "under the carpet," and eventually accumulated and became a "bump" with negative results.

Finally, mostly through trial and error, we realized that we see the world through very different lenses. Years later, our son Greg remarked that "the difference between Mom and Dad is that Mom sees the forest, but Dad sees the bark on the tree!"

Recently, we took the Myers-Briggs Type Indicator (MBTI) test, which confirmed just how different we are. This is an instrument used to bring personality differences to light. It exposes fundamental preferences in how we focus our attention and energy, take in information, make decisions and complete tasks to achieve goals.

The more similarities there are, the less potential there is in the relationship for conflict. As we learned, though, once couples learn to negotiate and capitalize on those differences, they can also be a source of richness and strength for the relationship.

Although it isn't possible to present the entire MBTI test here, following is a quick exercise to give you some idea of how these differences might pose challenges—and present potential strengths—for your relationship.

■

Exercise 1
BOTH SPOUSES

To get some idea of your personality type, put a checkmark next to the statements below that best describe you in each of the following four sections. Then choose the style in each category where you have the greatest number of check marks. Your spouse should do the same (using a different-colored pen if you are sharing one copy of the book). Important: There are no right or wrong answers!

CATEGORY #1:
HOW DO YOU FOCUS YOUR ATTENTION AND ENERGY?

Extraverted (E)
A people person who feels comfortable with lots of people.

Has many acquaintances; can feel deprived when isolated from people.

Externally motivated by people and situations.

Introverted (I)
Less sociable and more reserved.

Needs "private time"; prefers to know a few people well.

More motivated by personal values than by situations or others' expectations.

Check which fits you best – Extraversion or Introversion?
_____E _____I

CATEGORY #2:
HOW DO YOU TAKE IN INFORMATION?

Sensing (S)
Starts with experience and facts, then forms a global perspective.

Practical; "bottom line" person.

Intuitive (N)
Uses imagination and creativity, interested in the new and different.

Likes to be a "big picture person."

Uncomfortable with "fuzzy" information and ambiguity.	Comfortable with ambiguous situations.
A "now" person.	A visionary who tends to focus on the future.

Check with fits you best – Sensing or Intuitive?   _____S _____N

CATEGORY #3:
HOW DO YOU MAKE DECISIONS?

Thinking (T)
Uses logic and facts in decision-making.

Feeling (F)
Considers personal feelings and how decisions will affect other people.

Concerned about tasks and work to be done.

Concerned mostly about people's needs and reactions.

Skilled at being objective and analytical.

Skilled at gaining group input and consensus.

Sees conflict as inevitable and natural.

Uncomfortable with disharmony and conflict.

Check which fits you best – Thinking or Feeling? _____T _____F

CATEGORY #4:
HOW DO YOU COMPLETE TASKS TO ACHIEVE YOUR GOALS?

Judging (J)
Makes detailed plans before acting on projects.

Perceiving (P)
Comfortable without advance planning; enjoys spontaneity.

Methodical; prefers being well ahead of deadlines.

Works well under time pressure.

Likes a step-by-step approach; completes tasks before moving on.

Enjoys variety and multitasking.

| Manages life by using routines and target dates. | Prefers to avoid commitments that prevent flexibility and variety. |

Check which fits you best – Judging or Perceiving? _____J _____P

Husband's four personality type letters: 1.____ 2.____ 3.____ 4. ____

Wife's four personality type letters: 1.____ 2.____ 3.____ 4. ____

What do you do with this information? First, review the following "Opportunities and Obstacles" chart below, studying the four pairings indicated by the personality type letters you filled in above for both spouses. For example, if

| HUSBAND'S PERSONALITY TYPE IS: | 1. E | 2. N | 3. T | 4. J |
| WIFE'S PERSONALITY TYPE IS: | 1. I | 2. S | 3. T | 4. P |

You would study these four pairings below: E+I, N+S, T+T, J+P

PERSONALITY TYPE OPPORTUNITIES & OBSTACLES FOR MARRIED COUPLES

Pairing	Opportunities	Obstacles
E+E	We share many activities.	We forget to really listen to each other.
	We openly share thoughts and feelings.	We often interrupt each other.
	We like having people around.	We stay so busy there's not enough time for just "us."
E+I	We balance each other: I calms E, and E gets I to take action.	We enjoy different kinds of social activities.
	E handles our social calendar so I doesn't have to.	E wants "people time" while I wants more "private time."
	Before taking action E sees people issues to consider, while I points out ideas and values to consider.	E wants joint problem-solving discussion while I wants to process privately before discussing problems.

I+I	We feel very committed to each other.	We can assume our partner knows what we need, leading to misunderstandings.
	We appreciate each other's need for private time and space.	We don't share enough of ourselves to understand the inner emotional life of our partner.
	We both enjoy quiet, private time or time with a few close friends.	We need to develop more outside friendships.
S+S	Since we both live in the "now," we have a lot of fun together.	We often fail to make plans.
	We solve problems right away so life is less complicated.	Wanting to carry on our own family traditions can lead to conflict.
	We respect our spouse's need for stability.	We use tried and true solutions rather than thinking of new options.
S+N	When we talk, S is good at facts while N considers possibilities.	Our different perceptions of the world can cause conflict.
	N dreams and S figures out how to make these dreams reality.	S is concerned with "here and now," but N is concerned with the future.
	N can help S think creatively while S helps N be practical.	S thinks N should be more careful and precise; S's focus on details irritates N.
N+N	We experience deep commitment to each other.	We don't share enough of ourselves to know the "real self" of our partner.

	We both enjoy quiet, individual time, privately or with close friends.	We tend to avoid conflict until we have strong feelings about the issue.
	Even together, we can be "alone."	Not verbalizing assumptions can lead to misunderstandings and hurt feelings.
T+T	We agree on how to solve problems.	We have trouble expressing feelings and dealing with our spouse's emotions.
	Our needs for affection and intimacy are similar.	We often forget to express appreciation to our partner.
	We rarely have hurt feelings.	Our relationship can lack depth and be "robotic."
F+F	We express emotions and are considerate of each other.	When our values differ, we have trouble resolving the problem.
	We create a warm atmosphere that feels good.	Our choices may "feel right" without considering long-term consequences.
	Both of us enjoy activities that involve other people.	We hate disagreement so we "stuff" feelings to maintain harmony.
T+F	T adds objectivity when F feels hurt; F helps when T is confused.	T wants to solve the problem while F cares about relationships and harmony.
	F is sensitive to other people, while T can be "tough" if needed.	T thinks F is too emotional or subjective so can lose respect for the partner.
	T's logic balances the emotions of F.	We differ about how to add romance to our marriage.

J+J	Our home is organized and tasks get done as needed.	Our relationship can be rigid and have little spontaneity.
	We make decisions quickly.	Power struggles can happen.
	We enjoy a stable home and family.	Our conflicting ideas about how things should be organized can cause conflict.
J+P	P adds fun and J adds discipline to the relationship.	P feels constricted by J's serious side and unwillingness to change.
	J keeps life mapped out while P adds adventure.	J feels irritated over P's unwillingness to plan and can see P as irresponsible.
	While P makes plans, J helps implement these plans.	J is afraid P won't get a job done, while P is afraid J will always add more jobs.
P+P	Play is important to our relationship.	Our home can be disorganized or messy because tasks aren't done.
	We love creativity, change and flexibility.	One person seems stuck with decisions since neither of us likes making them.
	We have many options and alternatives in deciding what to do.	We both dislike child discipline so we may give in when we should say no.

Now have a frank discussion of how these Opportunities and Obstacles impact you, focusing on the following questions:

1. Which opportunities and obstacles apply to our marriage?

2. In what situations do the differences cause disagreement?

3. How are these disagreements usually resolved?

4. How will we change the way we make decisions (to minimize the obstacles)?

5. How can we ensure that both our needs are met?

6. How can we make the most of our strengths?

7. In what ways do our similarities limit us?

8. How will we change the ways we do things to compensate for the limitations due to our style differences, and make the most of the opportunities?

(Suggestion: More information about the Myers-Briggs Type Indicator is available online.)

#2 – *Leaving and Cleaving: Building Blocks of Unity*
The goal of "leaving and cleaving" is unity between husband and wife. God commands children to honor their father and mother. But upon marriage God expects us to give more honor to our spouse and to form a more intimate bond than we ever had with our parents. When the bride's father "gives her away" during the marriage ceremony, he literally gives his new son-in-law the devotion and loyalty she once had for her parents alone.

We've observed that in many troubled marriages a spouse's primary emotional attachment remains with one or both parents (or a sibling). This puts the other spouse in the difficult position of having to compete for attention, and making decisions and resolving disagreements are complicated by the parent's opinions or preferences. If the couple lives with the husband's or wife's parents, "leaving" is even more difficult to accomplish. Even if the couple has established their own household some distance away, if loyalties were never transferred, the bride or groom has not really "left" the family of origin, preventing them from taking the next step—cleaving to their spouse to create the unity God intended.

In other words, "leaving" is necessary for "cleaving" to occur. What does "cleaving" mean? The dictionary defines "cleave" as "stand by" or "stick to." Likewise, the Hebrew word *dabhak*, translated "cleave" in English, means to "adhere to" or "join to oneself."

This brings to mind the words of Jesus: "Therefore what God has joined together, let man not separate" (Matthew 19:6). This emphasizes that it is *God* (not we) who blends us together. By a mysterious act of God, we are now able to become "one flesh," suggesting not only sexual union but emotional unity as well.

Clearly, there are many other aspects to building unity in a marriage. We will cover some of these in future chapters.

Exercise 2
BOTH SPOUSES

Discuss the following questions with your spouse:

1. Are both of us more devoted to each other than to our parents or siblings? What is the evidence that this is so?

2. Who has a greater influence on our decisions: our parents or each other? Give an example.

3. If a parent criticizes your spouse, how do you handle it? Have you had this experience? What happened?

4. If you have had problems with your family making negative comments about your spouse, have you communicated to them that concerns about your marriage will only be listened to if both of you are present?

#3 – *Naked and Exposed: Getting to Know Your 'Real' Spouse*
The writer of Genesis tells us that Adam and Eve were naked, but "they felt no shame." Most of us think they must have been cavorting around in the garden, enjoying each other's bodies whenever the urge presented itself. Maybe that's part of the picture (and, in a perfect world, Eve's desire would have perfectly matched her husband's!).

Also, the climate in the garden must have been completely comfortable because they required no clothing for defense against the cold or heat. They weren't concerned about impressing anyone, so they needed nothing for making themselves more beautiful. Most importantly, they were completely innocent. As Matthew Henry's *Unabridged Commentary* says, "They had no sin on their consciences, so they had no shame in their faces though they had no clothes on their backs."[1]

But we think it's also helpful to consider their nakedness in a less literal sense. In a perfect marriage, people are completely open. They are vulnerable and trusting, exposing their thoughts and feelings and, since the Garden, fears and temptations and sins without worry of reprisal, rejection or criticism. In a word, they are *humble* with each other. Isn't that the spirit Jesus wants us to have all the time? We admit that we don't know it all and don't do everything right ourselves, so we can have a humble spirit with someone else.

Only when the wedding bells are a faint memory do people really begin to know their spouses. No matter how long the courtship, what kind of premarital counseling they had, or even whether they lived together before marriage, they are still virtual strangers to their spouses in the beginning. God's way is the *only* way to really know each other and return to the vulnerable, trusting, open kind of relationship first experienced by Adam and Eve. And God's way rests on the spiritual poverty or humility that Jesus calls for in Matthew 5.

Why is humility so important? Humility requires us to focus on God rather than on ourselves. David wrote, "Those who look to him are radiant; their faces are never covered with shame" (Psalm 34:5). As long as Adam and Eve were focused on God, they experienced no shame. They were completely comfortable depending on God and trusting him for everything they needed.

But when Satan entered the picture, Eve stopped looking to God. Suddenly she was concerned about herself, becoming suspicious of God for having forbidden them to eat from the tree. In her pride, Eve wanted God's wisdom for herself. So she gave in to temptation, took the fruit, and offered some to Adam, who ate it as well.

Notice what happened next:

> Then the eyes of both of them were opened, and they realized they were naked; so they sewed fig leaves together and made coverings for themselves. Then the man and his wife heard the sound of the LORD God as he was walking in the garden in the cool of the day, and they hid from the LORD God among the trees of the garden. But the LORD God called to the man, "Where are you?" He answered, "I heard you in the garden, and I was afraid because I was naked; so I hid." (Genesis 3:7–10)

The sins of pride and idolatry (desiring to elevate oneself as God) resulted in Adam and Eve covering themselves with fig leaves and hiding from God. Then, rather than taking responsibility for their sin, they blame each other and the serpent. Eventually God banishes them from the beautiful garden where they lived in harmony with him and each other. Isn't this exactly what we often do when caught in a sin? We cover up and try to shift the blame!

Although it's too late for Adam and Eve, their experience has much to teach us about marriage in the twenty-first century!

Yes, we will continue to work and suffer until we eventually reach God's "garden" of heaven, but repenting of *pride* is a first step toward coming out into the open and returning to the vulnerable, trusting relationships where there can be true harmony. In other words, pride resulted in our separation from God and each other, but Jesus has given us a way to reclaim that state of harmony if we are willing to practice his beatitude teaching about humility!

Exercise 3
BOTH SPOUSES

Take some time separately to reflect on each of the following passages. First read through the verses:

> Jesus called them together and said, "You know that the rulers of the Gentiles lord it over them, and their high officials exercise authority over them. Not so with you. Instead, *whoever wants to become great among you must be your servant, and whoever wants to be first must be your slave*—just as the Son of Man did not come to be served, but to serve, and to give his life as a ransom for many." (Matthew 20:25–28, emphasis added)

> For by the grace given me I say to every one of you: *Do not think of yourself more highly than you ought, but rather think of yourself with sober judgment,* in accordance with the measure of faith God has given you. (Romans 12:3, emphasis added)

> If you have any encouragement from being united with Christ, if any comfort from his love, if any fellowship with the Spirit, if any tenderness and compassion, then make my joy complete by being like-minded, having the same love, being one in spirit and purpose. Do nothing out of selfish ambition or vain conceit, but *in humility consider others better than*

yourselves. Each of you should look not only to your own interests, but also to the interests of others.

Your attitude should be the same as that of Christ Jesus.

> Who, being in very nature God,
>> did not consider equality with God something to be
>> grasped,
> but made *himself nothing,*
>> *taking the very nature of a servant,*
> being made in human likeness.

(Philippians 2:1–7, emphasis added)

Therefore, as God's chosen people, holy and dearly loved, *clothe yourselves with compassion, kindness, humility, gentleness and patience.* (Colossians 3:12, emphasis added)

Bear with each other and *forgive whatever grievances* you may have against one another. Forgive *as the Lord forgave you.* (Colossians 3:13, emphasis added)

Answer the following questions either generally speaking of all the passages or specifically of one certain passage:

1. Would people say this passage describes me?

2. What are some examples of how I am (or am not) like the characteristics listed?

3. What can I do to become more humble in this/these area(s)?

After completing this exercise individually, discuss your answers with your spouse. Encourage openness and vulnerability by being compassionate and gentle with each other.

The Impact of Humility

In his classic essay *Humility: The Beauty of Holiness,* Andrew Murray describes the amazing impact true humility will have on our relationships. One of his most convicting statements is

the following: "Humility towards men will be the only sufficient proof that our humility before God is real." If we want to
grow in our marriages (and be blessed with the kingdom of
heaven), humility is the place to begin.

In fact, the first step in becoming a more loving person is to
fully accept the fact that *we are not loving!* When we humble
ourselves so that God can infuse us with his loving Spirit, he
will begin to transform our character. We become more loving
because love comes from—is a "fruit of"—his Holy Spirit. Genuine love can't come from sinful people any more than apples
could come from a cherry tree.

The kind of unconditional love Jesus demonstrated is simply
not within our nature. The *only* way to become a more loving
person is to humble out and obey God. This obedience begins
with a contrite heart, the subject of our next chapter, as we seek
to *imagine true oneness.*

chapter 6

Imagine True Oneness

"Blessed are those who mourn,
for they will be comforted."
Matthew 5:4

Christ's Beatitudes are progressive steps. If our goal is just to feel good about ourselves, we won't be motivated to develop a heart of spiritual poverty and to face how completely powerless we are to live by God's perfect standard.

Instead, spiritual poverty leads to mourning our sin or having a contrite heart—being broken-hearted. Facing how insufficient we are, now we *grieve* our spiritual condition.

"Contrition" is hatred of sin combined with the intent to overcome it through God's intervention. In fact, the word actually carries with it the meaning of being crushed by God's word: "Is not my word like fire," declares the Lord, "and like a hammer that breaks a rock in pieces?" (Jeremiah 23:29).

In this day of "feel good" therapies, this step is repulsive to many people. Even in the church, those who consider themselves "faith based" (rather than "sin based") find it very difficult to focus, even for a time, on their sinfulness and how utterly hopeless they are without Christ's redemption. But that is exactly what Jesus requires so he can bless us.

When he pretended to be insane to escape Abimelech, David wrote, "The Lord is close to the brokenhearted and saves those who are crushed in spirit" (Psalm 34:18).

In marriage this step is especially important since the more humbled we are by our own sin, the more patient and nonjudgmental we will be with the sins of our spouse. Similarly, Paul taught that "one in spirit and purpose" comes from imitating Christ's attitude of humility:

> If you have any encouragement from being united with Christ, if any comfort from his love, if any fellowship with the Spirit, if any tenderness and compassion, make my joy complete by being like-minded, having the same love, being one in spirit and purpose. Do nothing out of selfish ambition or vain conceit, but in humility consider others better than yourselves. Each of you should look not only to your own interests, but also to the interests of others.
>
> Your attitude should be the same as that of Christ Jesus.
>
> Who, being in very nature God,
>   did not consider equality with God something to be grasped,
> but made *himself nothing,*
>   *taking the very nature of a servant,*
>   being made in human likeness.
> And being found in appearance as a man,
>   he humbled himself
>   and became obedient to death—
>   even death on a cross! (Philippians 2:1–8)

When we consider others better than ourselves and mourn our pride and selfishness, we can begin to *imagine true oneness.*

What Can Your Marriage Become?

> Now faith is being sure of what we hope for and certain of what we do not see. (Hebrews 11:1)

What do you *hope for* in your marriage? How will you grow to be "one in spirit and purpose"? How will your marriage glorify God while reflecting your unique gifts, personalities and lifestyle? Visualize your marriage ten years from now. Are you walking hand in hand into the sunset with upraised faces full of reverence and joy? Maybe you're serving with your children in a soup kitchen. Are you creatively acting out a lesson together to inspire your children's ministry class? Perhaps you're teaching a class of newly marrieds or hosting a Bible study in your neighborhood. Maybe you imagine kneeling together in prayer.

Exhorting his disciples to have faith, Jesus said, "Whatever you ask for in prayer, believe that you have received it, and it will be yours" (Mark 11:24). In other words, God will fulfill your dream if you simply believe, with gratitude, that he *has already given you* what you hope for!

The following exercise will help you zero in on that marriage dream, which will then enable you to be unified in your prayer life and spiritual preparation.

◘
Exercise 4
BOTH SPOUSES

Working in your notebooks, write a description of how you visualize your marriage ten years from now. Don't worry about what may be "realistic" based on your spirituality or relationship right now. Instead, be creative and *faithful* that God passionately longs to give you that full life Jesus talked about (John 10:10).

When you've both completed this exercise, share your answers with each other.

Working together, craft a description of your marriage, as if a decade had passed and this is where you are today. Make it as long as you like, beginning as follows:

"We're _____."

Then discuss:

1. What are the sins or habits we will need to change for our dream to become a reality?

2. In what areas will we need help from spiritual friends?

3. What new knowledge or skills can we develop to prepare for our dream?

Who Is Your God?

> "You shall have no other gods before me." (Exodus 20:3)

Selfishness, putting self above God, involves idolatry—the first (and most fundamental) sin God addressed in the Ten Commandments. Along with its "cousin" pride, selfishness is probably the most human—and the most destructive—sin we contend with in marriage.

Immediately after warning his disciples about the suffering he was about to undergo, Jesus revealed the cross that they must shoulder if they chose to continue to follow him:

> Then he said to them all:
>
> "If anyone would come after me, he must deny himself and take up his cross daily and follow me. For whoever wants to

save his life will lose it, but whoever loses his life for me will save it. What good is it for a man to gain the whole world, and yet lose or forfeit his very self?" (Luke 9:23–25)

Jesus' number one qualification for discipleship was self-denial. Self-denial is not only necessary for a strong relationship with God; it is essential for a strong marriage. Self-denial can improve your relationship by helping you to

- serve and sacrifice for each other;

- accept the weaknesses of each other;

- understand each other.

Serving and Sacrificing

Anticipating and meeting each other's needs is a building block of every strong marriage. To serve each other, though, requires the humility to set aside, or sacrifice, our own needs for a time. Here are a few examples from our marriage:

- Although Joy is the one who cares that the bed is made each day, when she leaves early, Adam makes the bed because he knows this is important to her. On the other hand, it is much more important to Adam that we arrive at events exactly on time (or early). Joy laughs about the fact that Adam "has her trained," but we have learned (the hard way!) that the minor inconvenience it takes Joy to satisfy this need makes for a much more harmonious marriage.

- There are many times when each of us will set aside a favorite activity to discuss an issue that is important to the other. And, if either of us is feeling the need for more quality time together, we are both quick to make this a priority.

- When it comes to media, we have very different tastes. This presents an opportunity to "trade off," so that both of us can enjoy our favorite types of movies or TV shows. (Adam now actually enjoys an occasional romantic movie, and Joy has learned to like "action" films.)

- We also take on "each other's jobs" as necessary—with Adam cleaning the bathroom, running the vacuum, or loading the dishwasher, and Joy going to the bank, taking out the trash, or paying the bills. These little jobs are a small price to pay for a smoothly functioning life!

- If one of us is ill, the other spouse will take on all the household duties for a time, as well as nurse the sick spouse back to health.

- In our intimate relationship, on the occasions that one of us is unable to perform using our favorite methods, we always find a way to meet the spouse's need. Not only has this flexibility and giving spirit always been a great strength in our relationship, it has also kept our sexual intimacy vibrant throughout our many years as husband and wife.

Your turn!

◨

Exercise 5
BOTH SPOUSES

Working separately, write your answers to the following questions and then discuss with your spouse:

1. In what ways do I serve and sacrifice for my spouse, foregoing my own preferences or convenience to meet his or her needs?

2. In what new ways can I serve and sacrifice to make life more pleasant for us both, and to enhance and strengthen our marriage relationship?

Accepting Weaknesses

None of us is without weaknesses and flaws. These can present a huge obstacle to marital intimacy or simply a tiny "blip" on the radar screen of life. This depends on our willingness to mourn and repent of our irritability, denying our selfish desires to overlook the things our partner cannot change, while gently communicating our concerns in those areas he or she can.

Most of us were "on our best behavior" before marriage. She wears her makeup; he "wines and dines" her; she cooks his favorite recipes; he closes the bathroom door and sprays with air freshener! Then the wedding day comes. Now they experience their partner "au naturel"—in the glory of early-morning bad breath, uncombed hair, toenail clippings, tattered old PJs, body sounds and smells. Has their romantic fantasy become a real-life nightmare?

In working with married couples, the following is one of our favorite verses:

> Catch for us the foxes,
>   the little foxes
> that ruin the vineyards,
>   our vineyards that are in bloom. (Song of Songs 2:15)

Imagine this scene: Sipping a cool iced tea, you and your spouse are relaxing on your porch swing in the late afternoon sun. You survey your vineyard, suddenly noticing a little red fox darting in and out between the vines, here and there stopping to nibble on your grapes. "What a cute little fox!" you remark. Weeks pass. Now the fox is a permanent fixture in your vineyard, and before you know it, a third of your grapes are gone. The fox, once so cute, has become a pest, and you are determined to get rid of it before it completely destroys your crop!

Little weaknesses and habits may be "cute" or at least tolerable in the beginning, but after a while, they can begin to eat away at your marriage. These fall into two categories: things we can't change and things we can.

In a long-lasting relationship, there are certain "human things" which we simply accept and learn to ignore. Irritations can be minimized even with these issues if we truly care about our spouse's feelings. Being thoughtful might express itself by closing the door when using the bathroom, covering the mouth before burping, opening the car window or getting the air freshener to dissipate body odors, and purchasing a special pillow or nasal strips to alleviate snoring.

Things such as leaving the toilet seat up (husbands!) and taking up the entire bathroom countertop with cosmetics and jewelry (wives!) fall in the "can be changed" category.

Two "little foxes" that have challenged us are Joy's habit of collecting piles of paper (rather than promptly filing or throwing them away) and Adam's tendency to overlook the importance of celebrating special times like Mother's Day and Valentine's Day. It took some effort (and help from spiritual friends), but we've overcome these little foxes—and many others—in our relationship!

Your turn!

■

Exercise 6
BOTH SPOUSES

List the "little foxes" in your marriage—the irritations that "eat away" at your relationship. Put these in two columns.

Foxes to minimize and accept: Foxes to discuss and change:

Now spend some time together going over your lists. Encourage each other and work together to minimize or change each of the items you listed.

Understanding Each Other

One of the most striking qualities of Jesus was his compassion. Because he understood the unique struggles of each person he met, Jesus was tenderhearted toward them regardless of their sin or stubbornness. Developing empathy for your spouse—being willing to "walk a mile in their shoes"—is a huge asset for a strong relationship.

How can self-denial help you understand your spouse? Empathy requires us to stop focusing on "me"—my feelings, my needs and wants, my fears, or how my spouse's actions might affect me. Instead, we must ask ourselves, "What's important to my spouse? What does he (or she) need? What is he (or she) thinking and feeling? What fears are causing him (or her) to react this way?" Obviously, since none of us can read minds, sometimes the only way to get the answers to these questions is to *ask*.

Unfortunately, this kind of questioning is only successful if the spouse knows what they're feeling and why, and is willing to share that information! Here's a typical conversation between spouses:

> She: "Hi, Honey. I had a challenging day today. How was yours?"
> He: "Hmmm." (pecks her cheek and picks up newspaper)
> She: "Want to talk?"
> He: (Looking at paper. Silence)
> She: "Can I tell you what happened to me at work?"
> He: (Silence)
> She: (Louder) "Are you listening?"
> He: "Give me a break! Can't I even read the paper when I come home? People at my throat all day and now all I want is a little peace and quiet!"
> She: "What's wrong?"
> He: "I give up!" (Stomps out of the room, newspaper in hand, leaving his wife feeling abandoned and wondering what just happened.)

But here's how the interaction might have gone if the wife had practiced a little self-denial:

> She: "Hi, Honey. How was your day today?"
> He: "Hmmm." (pecks her cheek and picks up newspaper)
> She: "Okay. I can see you need a little time to unwind. Later I'd like to tell you about my day at work." (She leaves the room, her husband now deep into the sports page.)
>
> (Later, after excusing the kids from the dinner table)
> She: "Can we talk a little? I'd like to hear about your day and fill you in on mine too."
> He: "Sure. Mine was pretty rough. People at my throat all day."
> She: "Sounds frustrating."
> He: "Yeah—pretty stressful. The boss is wanting that report on Thursday, and I haven't been able to get the people in my area to turn in their stuff yet."
> She: "You must be worried."
> He: "Right. If I don't get it in, that'll look bad for our whole department."
> She: "It's really hard when you have to rely on other people for stuff, and they don't come through."
> He: "You can say that again! Now, how was your day?"
> She: "It was really challenging:...."

Setting our own needs aside takes the ability to delay personal gratification in the short term, but pays huge dividends in the long term. I (Joy) have come to believe that "submitting" to Adam means being the *first* to deny myself. When I choose the path of self-denial, Adam eventually responds by meeting my needs, turning our interaction into a true "win-win."

As a psychologist, one of the most important skills in my (Joy's) "toolkit" is the ability to actively listen. When we choose to set aside our own feelings, opinions and needs for a time, this skill can help us "get inside the mind and heart" of our spouse, in order to *really* understand.

Notice that in each of the following examples the response focuses on the thoughts and feelings of the *other*. Practice the following active listening skills the next time you and your spouse are having a "heavy discussion":

Paraphrasing statements:

"Sounds like _____."
 Or: "You believe that _____."
 Or: "To you, it seems like _____."

Reflecting feelings:

"Sounds like you feel _____."
 Or: "You must be feeling _____."
 Or: "You sound really _____."
 Or: "You're really feeling _____."

Parallel Lives

Every marriage seems to have its "dangerous territory"—particular ways the couple tends to drift off the path of oneness. Adam and Eve ran into trouble when Eve made a major decision, deciding to eat the forbidden fruit without consulting Adam. In our marriage, a sinful tendency is to live parallel lives, remaining side by side while each of us operates independently, "doing our own thing."

In this pattern, days can pass without our having a meaningful conversation. We have our own times with God without discussing what we're learning, and we allow distractions and busy-ness to interfere with praying together on a daily basis.

One of the ways we are overcoming our tendency toward independence is that, before making decisions that can affect our marriage spiritually, financially, emotionally, physically or sexually, we have the following policy: We both must agree 100%;

otherwise, we postpone the decision until later or choose not to do it at all.

Although we might think we can be close to God without being close to each other, John wrote that "anyone who does not love his brother, whom he has seen, cannot love God, whom he has not seen" (1 John 4:20). Since the root of an independent spirit is pride, and a prideful heart will always keep us from connecting with God, the truth is that we can never be unified with God without first being unified with each other. To get back on track we must acknowledge, mourn and repent of the sin of independence.

◪

Exercise 7
BOTH SPOUSES

What are some signs that you and your spouse are truly "one flesh"? Working separately, rate your marriage on a 5-point scale, with 5 being "completely" and 1 being "not at all."

Rating

1. United in mind (1 Corinthians 1:10) _____

2. Living in peace (2 Corinthians 13:11, Ephesians 4:3) _____

3. Submitting to one another out of reverence for Christ (Ephesians 5:21) _____

4. Loving each other as we love our own bodies (Ephesians 5:28) _____

5. Contending as one man for the faith (Philippians 1:27) _____

6. One in purpose (Philippians 2:2) _____

Now take some time to discuss these with your spouse, deciding which areas you would like to work on and what each of you can do to become more united in that area.

Earlier we mentioned "idolatry." All of the strategies mentioned in this chapter will help us develop vibrant, godly marriages... *if* we are willing to feel the impact of our idolatry—the ways we put *self* above God and each other. The goal is not to make us miserable, but to motivate us to develop "godly sorrow" leading to repentance (and ultimately God's blessing).

Having begun to face and mourn our marriage sins, we are now ready for the next step: *surrender to each other.*

chapter 4

Surrender to Each Other

> "Blessed are the meek,
> for they will inherit the earth."
> Matthew 5:5

What does it mean to be "meek"? The dictionary uses synonyms such as "compliant" and "yielding," but we find the idea of "non-resistance" most helpful. Someone who is non-resistant may have the strength to resist but chooses instead to surrender. Jesus is the supreme example of non-resistance:

> When they hurled their insults at him, he did not retaliate; when he suffered, he made no threats. Instead, he entrusted himself to him who judges justly. (1 Peter 2:23)

Jesus had the power to call on 10,000 angels, but as the well-known hymn reminds us, instead he chose to submit. Why? Because he trusted in God's care and goodness. Jesus saw his Father's will and plan as superior to his own, and for this reason he relied completely on God. For him, surrender didn't mean *giving up* anything; instead, it enabled him to *gain* the power of God! Along these lines, Paul writes,

> But whatever was to my profit I now consider loss for the sake of Christ. What is more, I consider everything a loss compared to the surpassing greatness of knowing Christ Jesus my Lord, for whose sake I have lost all things. I consider them rubbish, that I may gain Christ and be found in him, not having a righteousness of my own that comes from the law, but that which is through faith in Christ—the righteousness that comes from God and is by faith. I want to know Christ and the power of his resurrection and the fellowship of sharing in his sufferings, becoming like him in his death, and so, somehow, to attain to the resurrection from the dead. (Philippians 3:7–11)

If only we would view submission this way! Then we'd welcome opportunities to die to ourselves, knowing that what we gain in exchange is much more precious than what we give up. Against this backdrop let's now consider the quality of meekness in marriage.

The Surrendered Wife

> Wives, submit to your husbands as to the Lord. (Ephesians 5:22)

> Wives, understand and support your husbands in ways that show your support for Christ. (Ephesians 5:22 Message)

"Paul and Donna" are a couple in their 50s. Donna has been a faithful Christian for almost two decades, and Paul was finally baptized earlier this year. Although they are thrilled to be unified in a way that was never before possible, they are also struggling with some new challenges. Donna has a good working knowledge of the Bible and has spent years overcoming certain sins in her character. On the other hand, Paul is just embarking on his Christian journey. In an effort to be helpful, Donna has become Paul's teacher, mentor and leader.

We recently met with Paul and Donna to provide some biblical marriage counseling. Paul expressed that he doesn't feel respected by Donna. They had disagreed about a decision, and Donna admitted she hadn't been willing to budge. I (Joy) read Ephesians 5:22 to her and asked, "If Jesus had been standing there instead of Paul, how would you have responded?" Donna immediately understood.

Like Donna, I am a woman with strong ideas and convictions. The words, "as to the Lord," can be interpreted, "as you do to Jesus." Keeping this in mind helps me submit. Of course, some women might respond, "If my husband were like Jesus I would submit!" That is not the point. The verse doesn't say, "Submit to your husband *if he is like the Lord.*" We submit out of obedience and trust, remembering that obedience is how we demonstrate our love for Jesus (John 14:23-24). Here's how Peter addresses the same issue:

> Wives, in the same way be submissive to your husbands so that, if any of them do not believe the word, they may be won over without words by the behavior of their wives, when they see the purity and reverence of your lives. Your beauty should not come from outward adornment, such as braided hair and the wearing of gold jewelry and fine clothes. Instead, it should be that of your inner self, the unfading beauty of a gentle and quiet spirit, which is of great worth in God's sight. For this is the way the holy women of the past who put their hope in God used to make themselves beautiful. They were submissive to their own husbands, like Sarah, who obeyed Abraham and called him her master. You are her daughters if you do what is right and do not give way to fear. (1 Peter 3:1-6)

For many years I have prayed for "a gentle and quiet spirit" since this doesn't come naturally to me. The Message paraphrases these words "unanxious and unintimidated." Fear is the barrier we must overcome to develop inner quietness. That's why Peter ends his teaching to wives with the words, "do not give way to fear." As mentioned above, trust is the answer—knowing that God is with us, loves us and will work all things together for our good (Romans 8:28).

When Submission Doesn't Seem Fair

Like Donna, there are many faithful wives who have persevered in their marriages for decades. Some of their husbands are harsh, emotionally abusive, and addicted to drugs or pornography. Some refuse to work. Some show no interest in a sexual relationship. Others insist that their sexual needs be met on a daily basis but never reciprocate with even a gentle touch or caress. Some of these men are not even committed to their children.[1] For many of these wives there is little hope in sight, as their husbands continue to show no real interest in their families or in God. Should they continue to submit to their husbands?

The answer to this question is yes. God allows some to endure unpleasant circumstances, while others seem to have a relatively painless life. The Bible has much to say about perseverance despite affliction and testing.[2] One thing is sure: Submission should never be viewed as an exchange for good treatment or blessing. It is simply done because we revere Christ (Ephesians 5:21). On the other hand, as we'll discuss later in this chapter, many men respond to a wife's respectful behavior with more frequent expressions of appreciation, love and gentleness.

What should we do when, in the midst of painful circumstances, the future is scary and uncertain? What if we feel trapped in a life that is like nothing we envisioned? We must first be honest with God, who already knows how we feel. Remember that our compassionate God loves the truth and hears us when we cry, "God, where are you? Are you still with me? I thought you loved me. Why are you letting me suffer this way?"

Although we often ask, "How do I escape this impossible situation?" we should be asking, "How do I overcome my unbelief and despair?" In her book, *Calm My Anxious Heart,* Linda Dillow asks the following question: "Are you going to judge God by the circumstances you don't understand or judge the circumstances in the light of the character of God?"[3]

What Does Biblical Submission Look Like?

Now let's get a little more specific by returning once more to the well-known passage in Ephesians:

> And further, submit to one another out of reverence for Christ. For wives, this means submit your husbands as to the Lord. For a husband is the head of his wife as Christ is the head of the church. He is the Savior of his body, the church. As the church submits to Christ, so you wives should submit to your husbands in everything. (Ephesians 5:21–24 NLT)

Notice that verse 24 tells us to submit to our husbands *as the church submits to Christ.* So the question becomes, "In what ways does the church submit to Christ?" Scripture teaches us that the church

- adores (loves) him;
- reveres and respects him;
- serves him (and enjoys it!);
- obeys his words;
- helps him fulfill his purpose.

□
Exercise 8
WIVES

How do you love your husband in these ways? Complete the following statements:

Adoration and Love
I show how much I adore my husband by:
I will grow to show my love even more by:

Reverence and Respect
I show my reverence and respect for him by:
I will grow to show my reverence and respect even more by:

Serving with a Happy Heart
I enjoy serving him in the following ways:
I will grow to enjoy serving him by:

Obedience
I obey when he asks me to:
I will grow to be more obedient by:

Helping Him Fulfill His Purpose
I help him by:
I will grow to help him by:

On his website, John Piper writes,

> When sin entered the world it...twisted woman's intelligent, willing submission into manipulative obsequiousness in some women and brazen insubordination in others.... [This is not] what we find in Ephesians 5:21–33. Wives, let your fallen submission be redeemed by modeling it after God's intention for the church!... Submission is not slavish or coerced or cowering. That's not the way Christ wants the church to respond to his leadership: he wants it to be

free and willing and glad and refining and strengthening. Submission is the divine calling of a wife to honor and affirm her husband's leadership and help carry it through according to her gifts.[4]

If our submission is to be free, willing, glad, refining and strengthening, and if we are to "honor and affirm" our husbands' leadership and use our gifts to "help carry it through," we will need to be strong, spiritual women. Personally, I can only do this when I'm empowered by the Holy Spirit. This brings to mind the beautiful allegory found in Revelation:

> "Let us rejoice and be glad
> and give him glory!
> For the wedding of the Lamb has come,
> and his bride has made herself ready.
> Fine linen, bright and clean,
> was given her to wear." (Fine linen stands for the righteous acts of the saints.) (Revelation 19:7–8)

In this passage we see the bride of Christ, his church, preparing herself to be righteous by dressing in "fine linen, bright and clean." In the same way, we must make ourselves ready by cleansing (sanctifying) ourselves and putting on Christ (see John 17:17 and Romans 13:14). We do this each day by immersing ourselves in the Scriptures.

□
Exercise 9
WIVES

Reflect on the following questions to decide whether your relationship with God is your top priority and whether you are surrendered to (and making the most of your relationship with) God:

1. Think about the past month. During a typical seven-day period, how many days have you had a special time with God?

2. How is your prayer life? Are you praying every day? Do you feel connected to God at these times? Are you praying throughout each day about temptations, challenges and victories?

3. How is your Bible study? Do you have a conviction that God is communicating with you personally during these times? Do you know how to use your Bible to get help with your sins, temptations, challenges and doubts?

4. Do you frequently find yourself "going through the motions" during your times of prayer and reading, rather than fully putting your heart into it?

5. Are you *expecting* God to encourage, strengthen, convict and instruct you each time you open your Bible?

6. What spiritual friend will you choose to help you and encourage you in this area of your life?

The Surrendered Husband

Wives are not alone in their need to surrender. After Peter describes the meekness and submission of Jesus (1 Peter 2:21–25), he instructs the wives to submit *in the same way*. This phrase is again used as he begins to address the husbands (see 1 Peter 3:7). In other words, a submissive spirit is necessary for all of us, although submission will look different for husbands, as Paul explains:

> And further, submit to one another out of reverence for Christ .... For husbands, this means love your wives, just as Christ loved the church. He gave up his life for her to make her holy and clean, washed by the cleansing of God's word. He did this to present her to himself as a glorious church without a spot or wrinkle or any other blemish. Instead, she will be holy and without fault. In the same way, husbands ought to love their wives as they love their own bodies. For a man who

loves his wife actually shows love for himself. No one hates his own body but feeds and cares for it, just as Christ cares for the church. (Ephesians 5:21, 25–29 NLT)

Husbands must love their wives *as Christ loved the church.* Let's think about what this love looks like. Jesus' love is

- a sacrificial love (he willingly—and *joyfully*—surrendered his life for his bride, the church);
- a cleansing love (holy and clean, washed by the Word);
- a perfecting love, bringing out the best in his bride (without a spot, wrinkle or blemish);
- a gentle love (he lovingly cares for his bride).

■
Exercise 10
HUSBANDS

Write down how you cherish your wives in each of the following ways, and then how you can grow to be more loving:

Sacrificial Love
How do you sacrifice for your bride (your wife)?
How will you grow to joyfully sacrifice even more?

Cleansing Love
How do you "cleanse" your bride, using the Scriptures to encourage and strengthen and lead her spiritually?
How will you grow in this area?

Perfecting Love
How do you bring out the best in your bride?
How can you grow to encourage and inspire her even more?

Gentle Love
How do you lovingly care for your bride?
How will you grow to be more loving and gentle?

Returning to John Piper's website:

> Sin...twisted man's humble, loving headship into hostile domination in some men and lazy indifference in others. Headship is not a right to command and control. It's a responsibility to love like Christ: to lay down your life for your wife...the divine calling of a husband to take primary responsibility for Christ-like, servant leadership, protection and provision in the home. This passage of Scripture... guards against the abuses of headship by telling husbands to love like Jesus: Husbands, let your fallen headship be redeemed by modeling it after God's intention for Christ![5]

If we husbands are going to love like Christ, following his example of servant leadership, we must allow his Spirit to control and live through us each day. Whenever we are tempted to dominate or be indifferent, we need God's word as our spiritual sword (Ephesians 6:17).

Exercise 11
HUSBANDS

Reflect on the following questions to decide whether your relationship with God is your top priority and whether you are surrendered to (and making the most of your relationship with) God:

1. Think about the past month. During a typical seven-day period, how many days have you had a special time with God?

2. How is your prayer life? Are you praying every day? Do you feel connected to God at these times? Are you praying throughout each day about temptations, challenges and victories?

3. How is your Bible study? Do you have a conviction that God is communicating with you personally during these times? Do you know how to use your Bible to get help with your sins, temptations, challenges and doubts?

4. Do you frequently find yourself "going through the motions" during your times of prayer and reading, rather than fully putting your heart into it?

5. Are you *expecting* God to encourage, strengthen, convict and instruct you each time you open your Bible?

6. What spiritual friend will you choose to help you and encourage you in this area of your life?

Love and Respect

Before we move on, we want to answer the question, "Does the Bible really offer answers for a troubled marriage?" After twenty years studying 2000 couples, University of Washington psychologist John Gottman learned to predict with 94% accuracy which couples would remain married and which would eventually divorce. In his book, *Why Marriages Succeed or Fail,* Gottman concluded, "Most couples I've worked with over the years really wanted just two things from their marriage—love and respect."[6]

Although Gottman studied couples from a wide variety of backgrounds, regardless of these differences, he found that, "No matter what style of marriage they have adopted, their discussions, for the most part, are carried along by a strong undercurrent of two basic ingredients: love and respect."[7]

We believe that couples with ailing marriages can trust the Bible for reliable help! As Peter wrote: "His divine power has given us *everything* we need for life and godliness through our knowledge of him who called us by his own glory and goodness" (2 Peter 1:3 emphasis added). This doesn't mean we should avoid getting help from more mature spiritual couples and, in more extreme cases, from qualified professionals. But it does mean that biblical principles can *prevent* us from getting into serious trouble in the first place. And when we *obey* the Scriptures, God is there to help us build strong, satisfying marriages that glorify him and inspire our children to become disciples of Jesus.

Getting Rid of Old Baggage

> "You must not bow down to them or worship them, for I, the LORD your God, am a jealous God who will not tolerate your affection for any other gods. I lay the sins of the parents upon their children; the entire family is affected—even children in the third and fourth generations of those who reject me."
> (Exodus 20:5 NLT)

Couples arrive in marriage with emotional "baggage" from the past. The impact this baggage has on marriage is often not within our conscious awareness. The following experiences are powerful examples of how this happens.

On one occasion we were in the car on our way to a meeting. Adam was driving, I (Joy) was in the front passenger seat, and our friends John and Pam Taliaferro were riding in the back seat. Suddenly I said to Adam, "Weren't you supposed to turn there?" Adam reacted with an irate, "I *know* where I'm going!"

John reflected, "Adam, you sound angry." Adam responded with, "I'm not angry." John reiterated, "You certainly sound angry." Adam insisted, "No, I am not angry." Pam offered, "Maybe you're not angry. Maybe you're bitter."

That evening at home we continued to discuss this very familiar pattern in our relationship. Typically, when I would "try to be helpful" (especially by backseat driving), Adam's anger would immediately flare up. I felt stung by his response. Since Adam couldn't explain why he reacted so intensely, we continued to talk about what had happened in the car. We wanted to figure out what it was about that kind of incident that "pushed Adam's hot buttons," since Adam is not generally a very angry man!

I finally donned my "psychologist hat" and asked, "When you were young, did anything happen that made you feel the way you do when I backseat drive?" After some thought, Adam explained that he often felt belittled by things his dad said, and his feelings during our interaction in the car reminded him of those feelings. My efforts to "be helpful" made him feel stupid, as if I didn't respect his abilities. This brought back painful memories of how he had been treated by his father.

This awareness reminded us of a conversation we'd had some years before. Reflecting on a recent argument, we realized that Adam's response to feeling hurt or threatened was to "put up an icy wall" of protection, a habit he had developed as a boy to protect himself from his father's harsh criticism. I responded to Adam's "wall" by pushing Adam for an explanation, which only resulted in him retreating more! Since I had felt emotionally abandoned as a young girl, the more Adam hid behind his icy wall, the more abandoned I felt by Adam, bringing back a flood of painful childhood memories.

We are so grateful God eventually brought all of this to light. As a psychologist, I (Joy) have seen many couples on the verge of divorce because of similar issues caused by "old baggage."

Exercise 12
BOTH SPOUSES

What old baggage did you carry into your marriage relationship? Discuss the following questions to decide whether your current "hot buttons" are a result of some hidden baggage:

1. Are there certain patterns that seem to repeat themselves over and over in your relationship?

2. Do either of you have feelings with your spouse that remind you of painful feelings you experienced with someone in your past?

3. Do either of you tend to overreact to certain kinds of experiences in a way that seems out of proportion to the situation? Are these feelings or situations similar to what you experienced in the past?

4. Do you feel unable to control your response when you are treated a certain way, almost as if you were "on automatic pilot"? Are your feelings at these times similar to a time when you felt (or *were)* victimized by someone?

We also encourage you to discuss your reactions to the above questions with a mature spiritual couple. This is helpful for several reasons. First, reflecting on these questions can bring up difficult memories, so an encouraging, compassionate friend can help heal old wounds. Also, it is beneficial to discuss volatile marriage issues with spiritual friends, especially since "many advisers make victory sure" (Proverbs 11:14).

The first three Beatitudes are the basics of a healthy relationship. Having laid this foundation, we are now ready to build a strong, godly relationship that will last throughout the years. And, since building always requires hard work, we must now *commit to grow in faith and love.* This is the subject of our next three chapters.

5

Commit to Grow in Faith and Love

Part 1: Spiritual Unity

"Blessed are those who hunger and thirst for righteousness,
    for they will be filled."

Matthew 5:6

Do you enjoy great contentment and satisfaction in your Christian walk, your marriage and your life? Throughout the Bible, God demonstrates his desire to bring us fulfillment. David writes that his "cup overflows" (Psalm 23:5). God longs to delight our souls with "the richest of fare" (Isaiah 55:2) and bless us so much we "will not have room for it" (Malachi 3:10). Jesus came to give us eternal life, but also a full life *now* (John 10:10), a "rich and satisfying life" (NLT). Paul describes our ultimate goal as spiritual maturity, becoming "full-grown in the Lord...to the point of being filled full with Christ" (Ephesians 4:13 TLB).

All of this sounds wonderful, but at what price do these good things come? Jesus simply answers that if we "hunger and thirst for righteousness," we will be filled. In other words, we must yearn to grow more in love with God, more obedient to him, and more Christlike in our relationships.

A Step of Faith

Are you ready to do whatever it takes to grow? To enjoy fulfillment in marriage, we must first *commit to grow in faith*. Write your reactions to each of the following statements. Reflect on whether you fully believe the statement. If the statement seems difficult (or impossible) for you to believe right now, be honest about this.

■

Exercise 13
HUSBANDS

1. God calls me to be committed to the spouse he has allowed me to have.

2. God will work through my relationship with my spouse to help me be more like Jesus.

3. God wants to give me humility so I can learn from my wife.

4. If I wholeheartedly trust and follow God's plan for marriage, he will bless me in ways I cannot even imagine.

5. God wants to heal and change my marriage.

6. God's plan for me to lead my wife and family is the best—and only—way to enjoy a truly fulfilling marriage.

7. My wife and I are precious to God, and he longs to bless our marriage.

8. God is listening to our prayers and working to bless our relationship (even when it seems he isn't doing anything).

□
Exercise 14
WIVES

1. God calls me to be committed to the spouse he has allowed me to have.

2. God will work through my relationship with my spouse to help me be more like Jesus.

3. God wants to give me humility so I can learn from my husband.

4. If I wholeheartedly trust and follow God's plan for marriage, he will bless me in ways I cannot even imagine.

5. God wants to heal and change my marriage.

6. God's plan for my husband to lead me and our family is the best—and only—way to enjoy a truly fulfilling marriage.

7. My husband and I are precious to God, and he longs to bless our marriage.

8. God is listening to our prayers and working to bless our relationship (even when it seems he isn't doing anything).

To have the marriage of your dreams, you must believe these statements. Why? Because your ability to pray for your marriage with faith depends on it! Jesus said: "Therefore I tell you, whatever you ask for in prayer, believe that you have received it, and it will be yours" (Mark 11:24).

___

■
Exercise 15
BOTH SPOUSES

Now it's time to share your answers. Decide whether you are comfortable doing this one-on-one with your spouse, or whether you prefer to include another spiritual couple in your discussion.

Share each of your answers and your reasons for answering the way you did. Also brainstorm ways you and your spouse can strengthen your faith in each area. Then commit to pray through each of these statements daily for the next week.

Toward True Intimacy

The next step is to *commit to grow in love.* The love relationship God wants for us mirrors the perfect unity of his relationship with Jesus (John 17:22). It is the essence of oneness—"a love relationship so tender, pure, and intimate that it is patterned after that of Christ for His church."[1]

Although those who refer to the "one-flesh marriage" of Genesis 2 usually refer to sexual intimacy, we believe God intends us to enjoy "unity times four": spiritual, emotional, intellectual and sexual.

◩

Exercise 16
BOTH SPOUSES

Take a moment right now to rate your unity in each of these four areas. Also, comment briefly about why you chose each rating.

1. *Spiritual Unity* (Reading the Bible and praying together, having spiritual talks, sharing spiritual goals)

   1   2   3   4   5   6   7   8   9   10

   Poor   Average   Excellent

Comments:

2. *Emotional Unity* (Openly expressing feelings, showing affection by giving gifts and serving each other, sharing fun times, feeling close to each other)

| 1 | 2 | 3 | 4 | 5 | 6 | 7 | 8 | 9 | 10 |

Poor   Average   Excellent

Comments:

3. *Intellectual Unity* (Sharing interests and perspectives, discussing ideas, having good conversation)

| 1 | 2 | 3 | 4 | 5 | 6 | 7 | 8 | 9 | 10 |

Poor   Average   Excellent

Comments:

4. *Sexual Unity* (Touching, showing affection, enjoying sexual interplay, feeling satisfied in the sexual relationship)

| 1 | 2 | 3 | 4 | 5 | 6 | 7 | 8 | 9 | 10 |

Poor   Average   Excellent

Comments:

Armed with the above information, you're now ready to grow in each of these areas.

Growing in Spiritual Unity

Why begin with spiritual unity? We believe that if you get this one right, all the other ways to be unified will come more easily! Spiritual unity might be considered the bedrock on which all the other aspects of unity are built (Matthew 7:24–27).

Often used in marriage ceremonies, the following passage provides a powerful illustration of spiritual unity:

Though one may be overpowered,
    two can defend themselves.
A cord of three strands is not quickly broken.
(Ecclesiastes 4:12)

We cannot know what Solomon was thinking when he wrote these words. Nevertheless, the powerful image of a cord of three strands is a perfect analogy for a married couple whose lives and relationship are completely intertwined with and dependent on God. To remove the third strand (God) would be to significantly weaken the marriage bond. We all know of couples whose relationship with God was not a priority and whose relationships broke apart when buffeted by life's storms, as Jesus warned:

"These words I speak to you are not incidental additions to your life, homeowner improvements to your standard of living. They are foundational words, words to build a life on. If you work these words into your life, you are like a smart carpenter who built his house on solid rock. Rain poured down, the river flooded, a tornado hit—but nothing moved that house. It was fixed to the rock. But if you just use my words in Bible studies and don't work them into your life, you are like a stupid carpenter who built his house on the sandy beach. When a storm rolled in and the waves came up, it collapsed like a house of cards." (Matthew 7:24–27 Message)

When God is the center of our lives, it is also more likely we will be part of a supportive spiritual family. The probability of marriage success increases when other spiritual couples are committed to help us through difficult times, praying for our marriage and family, and providing us with biblical counseling.

Spiritual 'Togetherness'

Notice that the cord analogy suggests that spouses each have their own individual relationship with God. To put it more simply, growing in spiritual unity requires two people who are growing spiritually.

We sometimes talk with couples who prefer to do their daily Bible study and prayer times together. Although reading, praying and discussing Scripture together each day sounds like a sure-fire way to increase your spiritual unity, this isn't necessarily the case. One downside of sharing your times with God happens at those inevitable times when your spouse isn't available. They may be ill or away on a business trip. One of you may be going through a spiritual crisis. And at the risk of sounding morbid, one of you is probably going to die first! That's why it can be dangerous to *depend* on those joint "quiet times." In fact, an important advantage of each partner maintaining his or her own individual walk with God is that both spouses can continue to bring fresh spiritual insights into their discussions!

Of course this doesn't mean you should *never* have a joint time with God. You might enjoy a personal, private time with God during the week, and then share your reading and prayer time on Saturday and Sunday. Whatever plan you choose, just be sure to include regular opportunities for individual Bible study and prayer so you can keep growing in your personal connection with God.

Tips for Growing More Spiritually Unified

Tip #1 – Live in the Light

> But if we are living in the light, as God is in the light, then we have fellowship with each other, and the blood of Jesus, his Son, cleanses us from all sin. If we claim we have no sin, we are only fooling ourselves and not living in the truth. But

if we confess our sins to him, he is faithful and just to forgive
us our sins and to cleanse us from all wickedness. (1 John
1:7–9 NLT)

Being unified means enjoying real fellowship with each other.
Synonyms for "fellowship" include "camaraderie," "companionship," "intimacy" and "togetherness." What we want in our
marriages is that "best friend" kind of closeness where people
feel they have everything in common.

John says this kind of fellowship comes from living in the light,
and in the verses that follow, says clearly that confession of sin
is an essential part of the light-filled life. But, besides God, to
whom should we confess? According to James:

Confess your sins to each other and pray for each other so
that you may be healed. The earnest prayer of a righteous
person has great power and produces wonderful results.
(James 5:16 NLT)

To some, confessing sin to another person (even our spouse)
may seem awkward or embarrassing. But prayer usually includes confession (Matthew 6:9–13), so spouses who pray together find that vulnerability comes easier.

When we have nothing to hide or prove to our spouses because
they know and love the person we *really* are—flaws and all—we
are able to relax, feel secure and support each other in becoming the person God created us to be.

Unfortunately, because our society implicitly teaches that
"macho" equals manliness, vulnerability is often more difficult
for husbands to express. But when these "macho men" become
more humble, soft and vulnerable, they often find their wives
responding with great compassion and, let's admit it, sexual
interest!

◨

Exercise 17
BOTH SPOUSES

In your personal prayer times, talk to God about the following questions, jotting down in your notebook any feelings and thoughts that come to mind. Then decide whether you feel comfortable discussing your feelings and thoughts about each question alone with your spouse, or whether the discussion might go more smoothly in the presence of another spiritual couple. Share this decision with each other, committing beforehand that if one of you prefers to include another couple, you will both agree to this decision.

To prevent the common tendency to blame our spouse (Matthew 7:3–5), the following questions focus on how husband and wife can each take personal responsibility for increasing the level of spiritual intimacy in the relationship.

Consider (and then discuss) the following questions:

1. Am I satisfied with our level of camaraderie and companionship?

2. Are there indicators that we are not as close as we could be?

3. Am I really walking in the light?

4. Are there sins or areas of my life that I am concerned about sharing with my spouse? If so, am I afraid to be vulnerable with my spouse? Why?

5. If I hesitate to confess certain sins, why is this true? What do I imagine might happen if I were completely vulnerable and open?

6. What can I do personally to increase our level of fellowship, vulnerability and intimacy?

Tip #2 – Pray Together Daily

> "Again, I tell you that if two of you on earth agree about anything you ask for, it will be done for you by my Father in heaven. For where two or three come together in my name, there am I with them." (Matthew 18:19–20)

Do you really believe this passage? Do you *act* as if you believe it? How can we say we believe Jesus' words if we do not pray together regularly? When we counsel couples, we always ask about this. Typically they react sheepishly, responding that, other than prayer at mealtimes, their joint prayers are hit-or-miss. They often explain that their lives are *so* busy and that they feel guilty about not praying together more often.

We definitely understand what it is to have busy lives. And, since there are times we drift from our commitment to pray together daily, we know what a difference it makes.

Here are ten of the benefits of praying together daily. In this list, we are specifically interested in the ways joint prayer will enhance your relationship. (We are not including all the benefits of personal prayer or the ways joint prayer can improve other aspects of your life besides the marriage relationship.)

- Since joint prayer moves God to action, praying together about your relationship is the number one way to improve your marriage.

- Your overall communication will deepen as you gradually learn to tune in to each other's feelings and needs.

- You can enjoy "intimacy without argument," since it is easier to *tell the truth* without fearing your spouse's reactions or reprisals during a prayer time.

- Joint prayer increases intimacy, which in turn will improve your sexual relationship.

- "All about me" becomes "all about us," reducing the tendency toward selfishness.

- God will provide direction and solutions as you pray together about challenges you face in your marriage and family.

- Joint prayer encourages spouses to be vulnerable—which then increases humility, understanding and willingness to forgive each other.

- Praying together is the best way to encourage and inspire each other.

- As you trust God by petitioning him to strengthen your marriage, he will begin to answer these prayers, helping you trust and rely on him for even greater victories in your relationship.

- Praying is contagious: The more you pray together, the more you will *want* to pray together!

In researching this section, we discovered some who claim that praying together is "the most intimate act between a man and a woman." This statement is controversial (since dating couples and other unmarried men and women also pray together), but we agree that having an honest conversation with God in the presence of other people is an act of profound spiritual and emotional intimacy.

This observation is supported by a study at the University of Virginia concluding that "shared religious activity—attending church together and especially praying together—is linked to higher levels of relationship quality."[2] In fact, a 20 to 30% elevation in romance, conversation and various levels of marital happiness was found in couples who pray together regularly.

Of course, the Bible makes it clear that there are certain conditions under which God is more likely to act:

Humility and repentance:

> ...if my people, who are called by my name, will humble themselves and pray and seek my face and turn from their wicked ways, then will I hear from heaven and will forgive their sin and will heal their land. (2 Chronicles 7:14)

Wholeheartedness:

> "You will seek me and find me when you seek me with all your heart." (Jeremiah 29:13)

Faith that God answers:

> "Therefore I tell you, whatever you ask for in prayer, believe that you have received it, and it will be yours." (Mark 11:24)

Unselfishness:

> When you ask, you do not receive, because you ask with wrong motives, that you may spend what you get on your pleasures. (James 4:3)

Obedience:

> Dear friends, if our hearts do not condemn us, we have confidence before God and receive from him anything we ask, because we obey his commands and do what pleases him. (1 John 3:21–22)

■
Exercise 18
BOTH SPOUSES

Discuss the following questions with your spouse:

1. Are we willing to make praying together a priority?

2. What are some ways we can improve our joint prayer life?

3. How can we pray together more often? Are we willing to commit to this?

4. How can we increase the vulnerability (honesty) of our prayers? Are we willing to commit to this?

5. How can we increase the length of our prayers? Are we willing to commit to this?

6. How can we increase the likelihood that God will hear and answer our prayers? Are we willing to commit to this?

7. Are we willing to start keeping a prayer journal where we list people and situations to pray for, including specific prayer requests for the following:
   - Our ability to fulfill God's vision for our marriage
   - Opportunities and effectiveness in serving together
   - Our sexual relationship
   - Our physical and mental health
   - Our finances
   - Our effectiveness in reaching others for Christ (including our children, neighbors and extended family members)
   - Our communication
   - Our conflict resolution
   - Our personal righteousness, purity and self-control
   - Our repentance in other areas that affect our marriage
   - Other issues unique to our relationship

Tip #3 – Serve Together

Meanwhile a Jew named Apollos, a native of Alexandria, came to Ephesus. He was a learned man, with a thorough knowledge of the Scriptures. He had been instructed in the way of the Lord, and he spoke with great fervor and taught about Jesus accurately, though he knew only the baptism of John. He began to speak boldly in the synagogue. When

Priscilla and Aquila heard him, they invited him to their home
and explained to him the way of God more adequately.
(Acts 18:24–26)

Priscilla and Aquila were a key couple assisting Paul in his ministry. Paul calls them his "fellow workers in Christ" and mentions that they risked their lives for him (Romans 16:3–4). But they are only mentioned *together* in the New Testament. This suggests that they worked more effectively as a team than either of them did alone. Can this be said of your marriage?

We find great satisfaction in serving together. Not only are these opportunities fun and rewarding, they are also growth-producing. Whether we are working side-by-side in children's ministry, helping another couple resolve conflict, participating in a Bible study, leading a discussion group, or teaching a class about marriage, we usually remark afterwards about how enjoyable we found the experience. And in helping others, we become aware of our own gifts and strengths, as well as areas that are ripe for growth.

◼

Exercise 19
BOTH SPOUSES

Discuss the following questions:

1. In what ways do we already serve together?

2. Are these experiences positive?

3. If serving together hasn't always been enjoyable, what changes can we make to improve our satisfaction or effectiveness in these situations? Who can counsel us or mentor our growth?

4. What special knowledge, gifts and strengths do we possess that God can use?

5. What opportunities for growth has God revealed?

6. In what new ways can we work side by side to use our talents?

Tip #4 – Share Scripture with Each Other

> Let the word of Christ dwell in you richly as you teach and admonish one another with all wisdom, and as you sing psalms, hymns and spiritual songs with gratitude in your hearts to God. (Colossians 3:16)

Some of our most memorable conversations have been about biblical characters and themes. Although we each usually have our own private time with God, one of us will often say, "Listen to this verse!" or "What do you think this means?" Then we launch into a discussion that brings us closer to God while enhancing our marriage relationship.

Here are a few ideas to make these times especially growth-producing:

- Use the particular passage as a jumping off point to look up and discuss other biblical passages with the same or a related theme.

- Make the discussion practical by applying it to your own lives, encouraging, strengthening and gently helping each other overcome specific sins and struggles.

- Let your conversation spawn other questions for each of you to study, turning a single passage into an in-depth series about a particular topic.

- Enrich your knowledge by sharing what you are learning with spiritual friends, inspiring them to study the topic and share their insights as well.

Exercise 20
BOTH SPOUSES

Discuss:

1. Are we talking about the Bible when we are at home and when we are on the road, when we are going to bed, and when we are getting up (Deuteronomy 6:7)?

2. If we aren't sharing scripture on a regular basis, what prevents us from doing this?

3. How can we make these discussions more frequent and more practical?

4. Do we need to ask another couple to help us enhance the spiritual unity of our marriage?

Now that we have laid our foundation, in the next chapter we will look at some tips for growing more unified emotionally and intellectually. Then in Chapter 7 we will consider growing more unified sexually.

6

Commit to Grow in Faith and Love

Part 2: Emotional and Intellectual Unity

To be emotionally and intellectually united is to *understand* each other. Not only is understanding necessary for effective communication; an absence of understanding is the factor that most often drives couples to seek marriage counseling. This mind and heart connection is essential if we want to enjoy the kind of relationship that fulfills our deepest human needs.

Tips for Growing in Emotional Unity

Now let's consider some practical ideas for increasing our ability to make that all-important emotional connection.

Tip #1 – Set Aside an Hour Each Week for a 'Coffee Chat'

> Understand this, my dear brothers and sisters: You must all be quick to listen, slow to speak, and slow to get angry. (James 1:19 NLT)

To say that life in the twenty-first century is hectic would be an understatement. In many marriages, spouses are much like "ships passing in the night"—rarely having time to connect with or even acknowledge each other. That's why it is essential to choose a special time each week for catching up—to discuss hopes, dreams and feelings.

Important: This tip is for couples who are able to talk without great hostility, intense anger or argument. A coffee chat is not the time (or place) for resolving conflict. If it is difficult for you to have a pleasant conversation without losing control, get some help *now* from a mature spiritual couple (or if you have already exhausted the resources in your church, call on a professional marriage counselor with a Christian orientation). But don't stop reading! Just skip this section and go on to the next tip! You can come back to this one later.

Exercise 21
BOTH SPOUSES

We encourage all other couples to set aside a weekly "meeting" where they can spend one hour of uninterrupted face-to-face time. You might sit on a nearby park bench, at a table at your neighborhood coffee shop, or a booth at McDonald's. (You don't have to drink coffee for this to work!☺) Put this time on your calendar for the next three months, and make it a priority (because your marriage is important). This is your opportunity to reconnect *emotionally*. Here are a few discussion questions to get started:

1. What do I really appreciate about my spouse? (Tell them!) Thank them for something they did in the past week.

2. How are we each feeling about our relationship? Grateful? Encouraged? Hopeful? Excited? On a scale of 1–10, how close do I feel to my spouse? Why am I feeling the way I do? (For example:

"Right now I would rate our closeness as a "5." We've had too much going on this week, and I've worked extra hours to finish that project at the office. I'm really sorry I wasn't there for you this week, and I want you to know I'll do better this coming week!")

If your answers are not completely positive, take responsibility for your own feelings by beginning with "I": for example, "I feel discouraged when _____ because _____." Do not blame your spouse, but adopt an attitude of collaboration. (Example: "I feel closer to you when we take a few minutes before we go to sleep to talk and snuggle. I would really appreciate your turning off the TV after the news so we can do that, and I'm willing to finish up in the bathroom by 10:30.")

3. Take time to dream together. What service has God put on your heart? Maybe you dream of studying the Bible with your neighbors or serving the poor in your community. Maybe you're excited about an idea you had for inspiring your children or teaching a class together at church.

4. Set a weekly goal to accomplish together. For example, decide to pray together or share an encouraging scripture with each other every day for the next week.

5. Note that this is *not* a time to argue or resolve conflict (see Chapter 10)!

Tip #2 – Identify and Develop Common Interests (and Enjoy Them Together)

> God said, "It's not good for the Man to be alone; I'll make him a helper, a companion." (Genesis 2:18 Message)

One of the best things about marriage is companionship. We have a great time together, no matter what we do! On our first date, we literally danced the night away. That was an activity we both loved (and unlike Joy's previous dates, Adam was good at it!). Since that night long ago (among other things), we have gone horseback riding, fishing, boating, water skiing and swimming; we have played golf and tennis, gone to art shows, played cards and dominos, traveled, hosted dinner parties, and eaten at *lots* of restaurants (since we both love talking over great food). What do *you* do together?

Maybe you enjoy camping, roller skating, bowling or playing Scrabble. Maybe you both love watching crime dramas at the movies or on TV. Maybe you like "cultural" things such as going to the opera or the theatre. Maybe you both sing in a choir or hang out at a dance studio. Sharing activities like these will cement your relationship.

Sometimes we visit with couples who report they "have nothing in common." How sad! Maybe they just haven't tried to find activities they both enjoy. Simply Google "recreational activities" to find hundreds of possibilities!

If one of you likes an activity that the other doesn't, be flexible. When our son Greg was young, we were very much a "soccer family." (Even as an adult Greg is such a soccer enthusiast that he proposed to his wife, Kristi, on a soccer field inside a soccer goal!) Adam also refereed and played on a men's team. And I (Joy) could have cared less about soccer!

I finally joined a women's soccer team (if we ever meet, please don't ask me about my *very short* soccer career!). However, I learned to enjoy soccer games, especially if one of my guys was playing. (I still don't really enjoy soccer games on TV.) Golf was different: I learned to play—and have had fun doing it despite my lack of skill.

Adaptability is the key when it comes to recreation. For example, Adam isn't crazy about going to plays but will go once in a while because I enjoy them. I'm not crazy about indoor sports, but I'll go occasionally. The point is, your marriage is worth a little boredom, and if you give yourself a chance, you may even find a new hobby you enjoy.

Identifying activities in common is important, but it is useless if you don't make time to actually *do them* together! Make it a priority to have fun together, not just because you enjoy it, but because it glorifies God. When people see your lives, are they impressed by your *friendship*—the ways you simply enjoy being together?

We have fun together whether we are grocery shopping or taking a walk or simply lounging around in our pj's! But we also enjoy lots of different recreational activities. Most important, we are both willing to try something new. What about you? Ask yourself whether the following verse describes your marriage:

> Our mouths were filled with laughter,
>   our tongues with songs of joy.
> Then it was said among the nations,
>   "The LORD has done great things for them."
> (Psalm 126:2)

Consider whether the following list includes activities you enjoy...or would be willing to try:

Sample Recreational Activities for Couples

Indoor games: card games, Scrabble, Monopoly, chess, video games, ping pong, air hockey, bowling, racquetball, karate, dancing, billiards, shuffleboard

Sports and outdoor games: tennis, lawn bowling, badminton, croquet, skeet shooting, snowboarding, golf, ice skating, hiking, running, sailing, skydiving, volleyball, skiing, mountain climbing, going to the beach/swimming, horseback riding, bicycling, ballooning, archery, fishing, surfing

Hobbies to pursue together: photography, gourmet cooking, stamp collecting, woodworking, model building, video production, acting, astronomy, bodybuilding, genealogy, ham radio, auto detailing, antique collecting/flea marketing, stained glass

Cultural activities: attending opera, theatre, art exhibits, museums, concerts and other smaller-scale music events

Sporting events: attending football, soccer, baseball, ice hockey games, horse shows

Volunteering: church work, serving in a soup kitchen, collecting for charity, working at polls during election, political action

Intellectual activities: studying history of the Bible or an era, book clubs, Sudoku or crossword puzzles

Lessons: salsa dancing, French cooking, watercolor painting, sculpture, ceramics, flying

Media: television, movies, collecting classic music

Travel: overnighters, weekend trips, historical tours, RV-ing, train trips

Home projects: decorating, remodeling, refinishing furniture, gardening

Miscellaneous: dining out, hospitality, shopping, camping, club memberships

---

◼

Exercise 22
BOTH SPOUSES

List ten different activities you would enjoy doing with your spouse. Don't include solitary activities like reading, unless you like doing these side by side, each with your materials. If you have trouble thinking of different items for your list, go back to the activities listed above and choose those you imagine you *would* enjoy.

When both of you have completed your lists, compare them. Look for activities both of you listed. Then look for activities on your spouse's list that you didn't write down but are willing to try. Schedule a special time, *at least once a month,* to engage in these activities together.

Tips for Growing in Intellectual Unity

"Trekkies" (*Star Trek* aficionados) will remember Mr. Spock's amazing "mind meld," the ability to fuse his thoughts with those of someone else. Unfortunately this power is beyond us, so we offer the following how-to's for boosting your intellectual connection.

Tip #1 – Discuss Ideas and Current Events

Understanding and respecting each other's opinions are important elements of any *friendship.* Jesus said his disciples were "friends" because he was telling them everything he had learned from his Father (John 15:15.) In the same way, we each have unique perspectives that help make us special, and while it isn't essential to agree on every detail of life (Romans 14:5), the more we know about our spouse's values and convictions, the more connected we will feel.

I (Joy) am less likely to read the morning paper, but every day Adam reads me the celebrity birthdays (we're not the only ones getting old!), and we laugh at his favorite comic strip. He'll also point out articles he thinks I'll find interesting, and throughout the day we discuss other items we read or hear about on the news.

None of this is intentional; we just enjoy sharing with each other. After so many years together we know each other so well, we finish each other's sentences!

■
Exercise 23
BOTH SPOUSES

Discuss: How often do we discuss ideas and current events? Do we feel the need to do this more? If so, how might we do this?

Tip #2 – Share Inspirational Passages from Christian Books

> Now these are the gifts Christ gave to the church: the apostles, the prophets, the evangelists, and the pastors and teachers. Their responsibility is to equip God's people to do his work and build up the church, the body of Christ. This will continue until we all come to such unity in our faith and knowledge of God's Son that we will be mature in the Lord, measuring up to the full and complete standard of Christ. (Ephesians 4:11–13 NLT)

Studying an uplifting book or article together—or sharing what you have found personally inspiring with your spouse—will help you grow in intellectual and spiritual unity! In the above passage, Paul says that this spiritual unity and knowledge are actually the building blocks for Christian maturity.

An unlimited supply of wonderful books written by evangelists, elders, teachers, and men and women with inspiring life experiences is available to provide spiritual help with almost any challenge you may be facing. Simply visiting dpibooks.org, Googling "publishers of Christian books," searching Amazon.com, or driving to your local Christian bookstore will reveal an amazing array of titles.

These resources can help you personally, in your marriage and parenting, evangelism, leadership and service. But our point here is that, by reading and sharing your thoughts with your spouse, you can grow more unified and effective in serving God's people!

◧

Exercise 24
BOTH SPOUSES

Discuss: What is our plan for sharing inspirational passages from Christian books and articles?

Tip #3 – Choose Mentally Stimulating Activities and Share Your Reactions

> "O my darling, lingering in the gardens, your companions are fortunate to hear your voice. Let me hear it, too!" (Song of Songs 8:13 NLT)

Are you like the young man in this verse, who loves to hear his lover's voice? Do you really respect and listen to your spouse's ideas and feelings? What activities inspire you to *talk* with each other?

Whenever we vary our normal routine—share a meal with friends, take in a movie, wander in antique (junk) shops, get together with our grandchildren, or enjoy a concert, we always reflect on our experience afterwards.

Eighteenth century poet William Cowper advised that "variety is the spice of life." This is especially true if you want to add spice to your spouse! Life is too short to live a humdrum existence, so we encourage you to explore the many opportunities for fun (even on a very limited budget).

◧

Exercise 25
BOTH SPOUSES

Discuss: What is our plan for enjoying (and discussing) mentally stimulating activities?

Having become more unified spiritually, emotionally and intellectually, we are now ready to develop a true "one flesh" relationship. How can we "spice up" our marriages, growing to delight in each other sexually? This is the topic of our next chapter.

Commit to Grow in Faith and Love

Part 3: Sexual Unity

Of all the couples we have counseled, very few have reported finding their sexual relationship truly fulfilling. While today's world may be light-years more advanced than the Victorian era, we continue to be amazed at the number of people who enter marriage with puritanical attitudes and inaccurate or incomplete sexual information.

God designed our bodies and authored the sexual relationship. We believe that this part of marriage is intended to glorify him and to bring us extraordinary pleasure and blessing. With that in mind, let's consider how to grow in our sexual unity.

Tips for Growing in Sexual Unity

Following are some specific steps that have helped our sexual relationship to become more exciting and satisfying.

Tip #1 – Become More Affectionate

> One night as I lay in bed, I yearned for my lover. I yearned
> for him, but he did not come. So I said to myself, "I will get
> up and roam the city, searching in all its streets and squares.
> I will search for the one I love." So I searched everywhere
> but did not find him. The watchmen stopped me as they
> made their rounds, and I asked, "Have you seen the one I
> love?" Then scarcely had I left them when I found my love! I
> caught and held him tightly, then I brought him to my
> mother's house, into my mother's bed, where I had been con-
> ceived. (Song of Songs 3:1–4 NLT)

In this passage, the young woman *yearns* for her lover. Then she
pursues him until she brings him to her bed. Do you yearn for
and pursue each other? This longing to be together, to be one
with each other, is the spark of sexual love. It will show in the
way you reach out and touch each other (even when sex is *not*
on your mind).

It is no secret that men and women are made differently! One
place this difference is apparent is the area of physical affection.
Wives will say they want to be "romanced into the bedroom."
What they mean is that, for them, sexual intimacy should be
the culmination of a long sequence of gradually more overt seductive moves.

This sequence, which can take a day or more, might begin with
something as inconspicuous as a special smile or brush against
the arm. The couple might then hold hands, or one spouse
might give the other a back rub. Little by little, these caresses
become more obvious and more private until, eventually, both
spouses are "ready."

In most marriages, though, this pattern is the exception. A wife
will frequently complain that all she has to do is innocently
brush against her husband, and he thinks this means she's in

the mood for love. The other common complaint is that, while husbands are often interested in physical affection only on the way to the bedroom, wives want cuddling and touching even when they're not planning to make love. Some husbands actually see this as evidence of their wife's insensitivity, saying that this kind of affection can leave them feeling sexually frustrated.

Because of the vast chasm that often seems to exist between men and women, we may wonder, "What was God thinking when he made us this way?"

Before we reflect on that question (which, of course, only *God* can answer fully), we want to discuss the kind of stalemate that some couples reach when they are unable to resolve these differences. One Christian couple we worked with, "Hank" and "Betsy," had been married fifteen years. Betsy claimed Hank had become more and more distant and uncaring, and Hank complained that she was "cold" and not interested in sex. She wouldn't give him sex unless he gave her emotional closeness. There they stayed, neither willing to budge.

I (Joy) suggested to Betsy that, if she would follow the biblical directive to submit to her husband in everything (Ephesians 5:24), he would probably come around and meet her needs too. So she began to "give in" to Hank—although not wholeheartedly.

Unfortunately, she tended to view these times as "prostituting herself," growing more bitter and angry. Although her submission succeeded in quieting Hank's complaints, Betsy never put her heart into their lovemaking, so there has been little real progress toward unity. Why? A selfish (unloving) motive will never produce a loving relationship, and heartless submission will never please God *or* our husbands. On the other hand, if she had submitted "as to the Lord" (Ephesians 5:22), perhaps the result would have been different.

Now back to the question, "If God wants us to have wonderful marriages, why has he made us so different?" Excellent books are available about gender differences, including John Gray's best-selling *Men Are from Mars, Women Are from Venus*[1] and Deborah Tannen's *You Just Don't Understand: Women and Men in Conversation,*[2] so we won't discuss these differences in detail. But why would our loving God intentionally create us with differences that seem to cause great trouble in marriage? Without launching into a long "academic" discussion, the following thoughts seem most helpful:

Although we tend to think of human differences as obstacles, they are also *opportunities.* How would we learn from each other if we were all identical? A man and a woman both bring something unique to a relationship, adding excitement, richness and variety. Women, in particular, were created to be suitable helpers (Genesis 2:18), giving wives the ability to add something useful to their husbands' lives.

Most importantly, God wants us to seek a relationship with him (Acts 17:27). Without relationship challenges, would we even see the need for God's help (2 Corinthians 1:8–11)? Without our sinful responses to the differences in others, would we see how much we need a savior? Would we seek to follow his direction in Scripture? We tend to be prideful and self-sufficient, even with the struggles we face. Without these challenges, we would surely see ourselves as gods!

How can we grow to express greater affection for our spouse? Here are a few suggestions:

- In most marriages, one spouse is typically more "touchy-feely" than the other. If you are that person, don't hold back—unless your spouse complains! In the early years of our marriage, I (Joy) had a very unhelpful belief: Since I needed more physical touch than Adam, I thought this meant I loved him more than he loved me. So I often resisted the impulse to touch Adam, thinking I should wait for him to touch me first. Now I know our marriage would have blossomed more quickly if I had given in to this natural impulse.

- You may differ in comfort with public displays of affection. If one of you strongly dislikes showing affection publicly, the other spouse must respect this wish. Find a level of closeness that is acceptable to both of you. For example, the husband who is uncomfortable putting his arm around his wife might be fine holding hands or simply sitting close together, upper arms touching. (And be sure to discuss *why* a spouse is uncomfortable with public affection, since this may uncover issues or fears that might be put to rest.)

- If showing affection is not commonplace in your marriage, try gradually adding little "touches." The possibilities include the following:
  - Using the foot to touch under the table
  - Giving nonsexual neck, back or shoulder massages
  - Giving hugs
  - Holding hands
  - Putting your head on your spouse's shoulder
  - Lying down with your head in your spouse's lap
  - Caressing the back of your spouse's hand
  - Kissing the cheek, back of the neck, forehead...
  - Cuddling and snuggling
  - Walking arm in arm
  - Stroking each other
  - Resting a hand on your spouse's leg
  - Holding one another
  - Reaching across a table to touch your spouse's hand

- ◦ Placing your hand on your spouse's shoulder
- ◦ "Eskimo kisses" (rubbing noses)
- ◦ Caressing your spouse when they are dressing
- ◦ Cheeks-to-cheeks (the back ones!)
- ◦ (You add to the list!...)

Have you ever watched a dating couple who couldn't seem to keep their hands off each other? Nonsexual touching can strengthen your relationship and ultimately improve your sexual intimacy. Try it—you'll like it!

◩

Exercise 26
BOTH SPOUSES

Discuss:

1. On a scale of 1–10, if "1" is Non-Existent and "10" is "Constant," what is the frequency of nonsexual affection in our marriage?

2. If we don't touch much, why is this true?

3. What can we do to overcome any hesitation or fear about non-sexual touching?

4. Which of the activities on the above list do we want to try?

5. If need be, are we willing to start small and start *today?*

Research shows that humans need touch throughout their life. Touch is related to physical health as well as to marital happiness and sexual fulfillment. The Scriptures are replete with examples of Jesus using touch to comfort, heal and communicate caring: He touched the leper (Matthew 8:3), Peter's mother-in-law (Matthew 8:15), the eyes of the blind men (Matthew 9:29–30),

Peter, James and John to calm their fears (Matthew 17:7), the ears
of the deaf man (Mark 7:33), and the children (Mark 10:13, 16).
Shouldn't we follow his example?

Tip #2– Talk about More- and Less-Satisfying Aspects of Your Sexual Relationship

> Marriage is not a place to "stand up for your rights." Mar-
> riage is a decision to serve the other, whether in bed or out.
> Abstaining from sex is permissible for a period of time if you
> both agree to it, and if it's for the purposes of prayer and
> fasting—but only for such times. Then come back together
> again. Satan has an ingenious way of tempting us when we
> least expect it. I'm not, understand, commanding these peri-
> ods of abstinence—only providing my best counsel if you
> should choose them. (1 Corinthians 7:4–6 Message)

If we are to "serve one another" in our sexual relationship (verse
4), we must first know what pleases our spouse. This may seem
obvious, but because of early experiences or beliefs about sex
being "dirty," many couples seem unable to discuss sexual topics without great discomfort.

We recall one couple who was having difficulty with their sexual intimacy. The wife had been married previously, and she assumed "all men" would like a particular sexual practice that her
first husband had enjoyed. So she was dumbfounded when her
husband rebuffed her efforts to please him in this way. Not sur-
prisingly, they had not really talked about their preferences, and
the wife was unaware that he had developed some negative as-
sociations with certain sexual activities due to a history of
painful sexual experiences.

As long as your discussions don't involve "coarse joking" (Ephesians 5:4) or mocking each other, *no conversation* should be
off-limits between husband and wife. Here are a few suggestions
for making these discussions more fruitful:

- Agree that it is acceptable for your spouse to gently guide you during lovemaking. This does not mean you need to stop, but rather that you will each indicate what you enjoy through non-verbal actions or quiet one-word responses.

- As necessary, find private, uninterrupted times to discuss your sexual relationship. Give yourselves permission to use whatever sexual terminology best communicates the information you need to share.

- Since our preferences in the sexual arena are heavily influenced by previous learning, we recommend that these times include not only your likes and dislikes, but also some explanation about why. Remember that the goal is to help your spouse better understand you. Here are some questions to answer:

  ○ Growing up, what taboos did you learn?

  ○ How did your parents handle discussions about sex?

  ○ What off-hand comments were made that created a particular impression about sex?

  ○ Was pornography a part of your past? If so, did you "buy into" the message that sex is about selfishness and power/control, rather than about love and giving?

  ○ What sexual experiences did you have during the dating years?

  ○ Were you ever sexually victimized (molested or raped)? If so, what feelings remain about this experience? Did you have an opportunity to talk through this experience with a supportive adult?

  ○ If you grew up in a religious home, what messages did you receive about God's view of sex?

◦ What did you learn from your same-sex parent? For example, mothers indicating that wives should "grin and bear it" in doing their sexual "duty" or fathers treating mothers (or women in general) with disrespect. Even subtle negative sexual messages can powerfully influence our later experience of lovemaking in marriage!

God created sex to be mutually satisfying. Think about it this way: If the "one flesh" marital relationship is to mirror the joyful union of Christ and his church (Ephesians 5:31–32), shouldn't our coming together be joyful as well? The bottom line is that God intends that lovemaking be pleasurable for both spouses.

When Sarah, who was later recognized as a godly woman (1 Peter 3:5–6) discovered that she was going to become pregnant again, she laughed and then remarked: "After I have grown old, shall I have pleasure, my lord being old also?" (Genesis 18:12, New King James). A sexual relationship between two growing Christians is designed for intimate *fellowship* as well as incredible physical pleasure!

Tip #3 – Add Times of 'Non-Demand Pleasuring' to Your Sexual Relationship

WOMAN: His face is rugged, his beard smells like sage, His voice, his words, warm and reassuring. Fine muscles ripple beneath his skin, quiet and beautiful. His torso is the work of a sculptor, hard and smooth as ivory. He stands tall, like a cedar, strong and deep-rooted, A rugged mountain of a man, aromatic with wood and stone. His words are kisses, his kisses words. Everything about him delights me, thrills me through and through! (Song of Songs 5:13–16 Message)

LOVER: Remind me of you, and I'm spoiled for anyone else! Your beauty, within and without, is absolute, dear lover, close companion. You are tall and supple, like the palm tree, and your full breasts are like sweet clusters of dates. I say, "I'm

going to climb that palm tree! I'm going to caress its fruit!"
Oh yes! Your breasts will be clusters of sweet fruit to me, Your
breath clean and cool like fresh mint, your tongue and lips
like the best wine. (Song of Songs 7:6–9 Message)

The couple in the above passages certainly know how to fully appreciate each other! If one thing can ruin your sexual relationship, it's the tendency to be goal-oriented. In other words, focusing on achieving orgasm rather than expressing your love tends to put pressure to succeed on both spouses. This pressure is especially harmful when "things aren't working right" for one of you.

Life stress, illness, hormonal ups and downs, medications and a variety of other physical and psychological factors can temporarily cause loss of ability to achieve orgasm. One bout of male impotence (erectile dysfunction) can result in insecurity and "performance anxiety" the next time around, further decreasing the likelihood of "success."

But what about the wife who is having difficulty? Of course, women can participate in sexual intercourse regardless of their level of arousal, but *enjoying* the experience can be difficult for many women, especially without accurate information about female sexuality. Women who are well informed are actually quite rare, even in this age where explicit sexual information seems to be everywhere. The lack of accurate information is likely more widespread in the church.

As we work with young couples in premarital counseling, we find many women who have absolutely no sexual teaching, which can certainly present challenges.

It is rare to find even non-churched women with positive, complete and accurate sexual knowledge. In fact, many have been promiscuous and have much to "unlearn." The bottom line is that, as always, God's way—arriving at marriage with "fresh eyes"—is still best.

Although married women can benefit from some very basic information about female sexuality (see Tip #4 below), one of the best ways to learn is to engage in sexual exploration *together.* This is what we mean by "non-demand sexual pleasuring." Sex therapists call this technique "sensate focus." In a nutshell, it involves giving pleasure to your spouse through a series of exercises involving six distinct phases, each lasting about an hour.

Consider the following:

> Sensate focus is an exercise that couples can do to enhance intimacy in their relationship. It is primarily used to alleviate anxiety related to intercourse. It is very effective in the treatment of desire, arousal, and orgasmic disorders. Typically, it takes 20–60 minutes 2 to 3 times a week for 6 weeks to complete the exercise.
>
> Each session should be carried out in a private environment without the possibility of interruption. Ideally, the couple should be completely undressed. If this causes anxiety, undergarments may be worn during the first stage. Create a romantic environment with music/candles.
>
> **Week 1–2:** The couple takes turns exploring the other's body and face. The genitalia and breasts should be avoided. The purpose of the exercise is to pay attention to tactile sensation. It is the individual's responsibility to tell the other person what feels good to them. Sexual intercourse and orgasms are not permitted during weeks 1–2.
>
> **Week 3–4:** Begin with week 1–2 exercises. Breast and genital stimulation are included this week. [Manual stimulation] and orgasms are also permitted.
>
> **Week 5–6:** Begin with week 1–4 exercises. Intercourse is permitted this week. Start slowly in a comfortable position. If anxiety or pain occurs, try going back to exercises from weeks 1–4 until an appropriate comfort level is gained in order to attempt intercourse again.[3]

This technique has helped countless couples overcome their sexual fears and difficulties. It can improve your sexual intimacy as you

- feel closer to each other and enjoy your sexual relationship more fully;

- overcome fears associated with sex—whether or not either of you was a victim of sexual abuse;

- learn to relax during sexual activity, since there is no worry about what to do, whether you will do it right, or whether your body will respond in the right way;

- discover what your spouse enjoys and how to give them pleasure;

- desire each other more;

- express your love for each other.

◩

Exercise 27
BOTH SPOUSES

Discuss:

1. Do we believe that our sexual intimacy is important to God?

2. Are we willing to pray for greater levels of sexual intimacy?

3. Are we willing to demonstrate flexibility and commitment to our sexual relationship by trying new things to achieve greater intimacy?

4. How much faith do we have that God will help us in this area? Remember that "faith is being sure of what we hope for" (Hebrews 11:1).

Tip #4 – Don't Depend on Worldly Myths About Sexuality

Buy the truth and do not sell it;
    get wisdom, discipline, and understanding.
(Proverbs 23:23)

Since we believe that sexuality is not a shameful subject and that accurate information is essential, we are going to be very straightforward in the following discussion. Remember, God created sex and called his creation "very good!" (Genesis 1:31). However, we apologize for any discomfort our readers may experience.

In the early days of our marriage, we didn't have the benefit of accurate information about sexuality. As a result, I (Joy) believed for years that there was something wrong with me. I assumed that, since I rarely experienced orgasm during intercourse, I must be flawed ("frigid" was the awful word I had heard people use for this condition). We were married almost twenty years when, during a graduate course in human sexuality, I finally learned that the inability to orgasm during intercourse is a *normal variant of female sexuality*. I was relieved to find out nothing was wrong with me, but by then I had endured twenty years of shame!

We have counseled many couples who have similar, incorrect and unhelpful beliefs about sexual intimacy. In the section that follows, we will attempt to dispel the most common of these.

MYTHS ABOUT MALE SEXUALITY

Myth #1 – The size of a man's penis is directly related to his wife's satisfaction with lovemaking.

Truth: Many men feel inadequate because, growing up, they came to believe that their penis was much smaller than other boys'. However, when erect, most penises are similar in size regardless of their size when flaccid (soft)—and men have little opportunity to compare themselves to others in an erect state. (Pornographic movies use media-enhancement to enlarge size.)

During vaginal intercourse, penis size isn't important: the outer third of the vagina contains most of the nerves. Even more important, the clitoris (rather than the vagina) is a women's main organ of sexual arousal, and it can come to climax no matter the size of the penis.

Myth #2 – Most men are always ready to have sex.

Truth: Although men have the reputation of being "oversexed," occasional lack of interest in sex is very common among both men and women. One researcher found that 30% of the men he interviewed admitted they saw sex as a "burden" at times. Sex can certainly be a satisfying part of life, but there are other things—even to men—that are just as (and more) satisfying.

Myth #3 – An erection is necessary for a man to enjoy sexual activity.

Truth: As mentioned above, being goal-oriented about sex means missing out on great pleasure. Your mind is actually your most powerful sex organ, and your skin is your largest one! Most men experience temporary impotence from time to time. This is to be expected and usually doesn't signal the end of "normal sex" (intercourse). During these times, couples can enjoy cuddling, kissing and using their hands, mouths and imaginations to give their spouses great pleasure in other ways.

When men pressure themselves to have an erection or worry about their performance, this only makes things worse. Sometimes men are reassured by consulting with a doctor, but remember that the most common causes of erectile dysfunction are fatigue, preoccupation with other things, alcohol abuse, prescription drug side-effects, illness, marriage difficulties, anger and lack of sufficient stimulation.

When a husband's orgasm is complete and he loses his erection, does sexual activity have to stop? Absolutely not! A couple can continue making love until both partners are ready to stop, and even then they may choose to spend time caressing and fondling each other, quietly talking and just *enjoying each other!*

MYTHS ABOUT FEMALE SEXUALITY

Myth #1 – 'Vaginal orgasms' are better than 'clitoral orgasms.'

Truth: This myth suggests that an orgasm triggered by a penis in the vagina is more pleasurable than an orgasm triggered by manual stimulation. This is not true. The clitoris *always* triggers female orgasms. On the other hand, it is true that the clitoris extends farther up into the body than originally believed, so some wives feel an orgasm more strongly when their husband's penis is within the vagina. But not every orgasm is a cataclysmic, earth-shattering experience (for either sex). Our advice is to just enjoy making love and giving pleasure to your spouse every time, regardless of whether stars explode!

We mentioned above that the inability for a woman to orgasm during intercourse isn't abnormal or even unusual. That's because the clitoris doesn't necessarily receive a lot of stimulation during sexual intercourse, so many women find more direct stimulation necessary to achieve sexual climax.

The other area of misunderstanding is "simultaneous orgasm." Somewhere we learned that spouses *should* achieve orgasm at the same time. Apart from the fact that "shoulds" are usually dangerous, research suggests that simultaneous orgasm is relatively uncommon. We strongly discourage couples from having this goal or expectation. As we said above, just *delight in* each other and the wonderful, warm experience of being "one," and enjoy whatever happens!

The bottom line? Everyone is different! That's why it's essential that you talk with (and show) your partner what you prefer.

Myth #2 – Women need an orgasm to feel sexually satisfied.

Truth: Women complain much more often about not feeling satisfied *emotionally.* For most women, lovemaking is more relational and emotional than physical. Many women can be satisfied without an orgasm if they feel cherished by their husbands. This is not to say that a woman doesn't enjoy orgasm, but simply to underscore that her orgasm means more when hubby is listening to her, caring for her and sensitive to her needs when they're *not* in the bedroom!

Exercise 28
BOTH SPOUSES

Discuss:

1. What did we learn from the above list of myths?

2. What difference will this make in the way we feel about our sexual relationship?

3. Are we willing to do something differently as a result of this information?

4. Do we need additional help with our sexual intimacy? What mature couple can we speak with?

The first four beatitudes provide rich opportunities for growing in our relationship with God. The result is that we also grow more Christlike, with a profound impact on our human relationships—particularly marriage. Now we are more ready to focus outward by imitating the mercy of Christ—to *overflow with compassion.*

chapter

8

Overflow with Compassion

"Blessed are the merciful,
for they will be shown mercy."
Matthew 5:7

People often ask the secret of our long-lasting marriage. This is a complicated question. Remaining married isn't just about longevity, but continuing to grow together through the years—enjoying a relationship that gradually becomes more delightful to God *and* both partners.

While there is probably no single secret to any successful marriage, we always answer with eight simple words:

Be Quick to Apologize and Quick to Forgive!

The 1970 movie, *Love Story,* ended with a hauntingly beautiful song claiming that, "Love means never having to say you're sorry." It would be difficult to find a happily married couple who agrees with this sentiment. Instead, part of being in a relationship means we will hurt each other. We will argue and need to resolve disagreements. We will sin against one another. And if we're to remain together, we will need to ask for and give forgiveness.

The Greek word Jesus used for "merciful" is *eleemon,* meaning "...feelings of pity, with a focus of showing compassion to those in serious need."[1] Taking the first five beatitude steps and acknowledging our tremendous spiritual need involves seeing ourselves as we really are. Compassion will overflow to each other as we ask ourselves, "Who am I to refuse to forgive my spouse when each day God so generously forgives the sin I repeat again and again, despite promising to repent?" (Matthew 18:21–35).

In his book *Taking the Word to Heart,* Robert C. Roberts addresses the destructive anger that can permeate so many relationships. He writes that forgiveness is

> at the center of God's therapeutic program in Jesus Christ, who comes to us as mediator, reconciler, unifier, healer of our broken relationship with himself and with one another. Jesus mediates to us God's forgiveness, thus making possible and necessary our forgiveness of one another.... The aim of Christian forgiveness is not to rid the forgiver of an unpleasant and disruptive emotion but to strive toward the attitudes and relationships characteristic of God's kingdom. Forgiveness is therapy, and love is the health at which it aims.[2]

For Husbands

Being compassionate and merciful means having the desire to meet our spouse's deepest needs. The Proverbs 31 "wife of noble character" must have done this well, since "her husband lack[ed] nothing of value" (v11). Some years ago I (Adam) developed a somewhat unconventional interpretation of this well-known passage. Although God may have intended these verses to inspire wives, I believe Proverbs 31 also includes an important message for husbands.

As the leader of his home, a husband is ultimately responsible for all that goes on within his doors. Although it's true that the Proverbs 31 woman is a veritable whirling dervish of good deeds, consider that she is able to be so spiritual and productive and fulfilled because her husband is doing something right!

Now reflect on the following verses, looking for clues to *how* she is able to accomplish so much:

> A wife of noble character who can find?
>   She is worth far more than rubies.
>
> Her husband has full confidence in her
>   and lacks nothing of value.
>
> She brings him good, not harm,
>   all the days of her life.
>
> She selects wool and flax
>   and works with eager hands.
>
> She is like the merchant ships,
>   bringing her food from afar.
>
> She gets up while it is still dark;
>   she provides food for her family
>   and portions for her servant girls.
>
> She considers a field and buys it;
>   out of her earnings she plants a vineyard.
>
> She sets about her work vigorously;
>   her arms are strong for her tasks.
>
> She sees that her trading is profitable,
>   and her lamp does not go out at night.
>
> In her hand she holds the distaff
>   and grasps the spindle with her fingers.

She opens her arms to the poor
>   and extends her hands to the needy.

When it snows, she has no fear for her household;
>   for all of them are clothed in scarlet.

She makes coverings for her bed;
>   she is clothed in fine linen and purple.

Her husband is respected at the city gate,
>   where he takes his seat among the elders of the land.

She makes linen garments and sells them,
>   and supplies the merchants with sashes.

She is clothed with strength and dignity;
>   she can laugh at the days to come.

She speaks with wisdom,
>   and faithful instruction is on her tongue.

She watches over the affairs of her household
>   and does not eat the bread of idleness.

Her children arise and call her blessed;
>   her husband also, and he praises her:

"Many women do noble things,
>   but you surpass them all."

Charm is deceptive, and beauty is fleeting;
>   but a woman who fears the LORD is to be praised.

Give her the reward she has earned,
>   and let her works bring her praise at the city gate.
(Proverbs 31:10–31)

I believe that this husband is creating an *environment* in which his wife can flourish. Look at verse 25: "She can laugh at the days to come." This woman is very secure. She has no doubt she is loved and no worries about the future. In verse 28 we learn that "her children call her blessed and her husband praises her." This man not only ensures that their children show consideration to his wife, but he openly demonstrates his appreciation and admiration for her.

Also consider that this woman's husband isn't threatened by his wife's success. Unlike the man we once knew who forbade his wife to get a master's degree because she would surpass his education, the Proverbs 31 husband appreciates and encourages his wife's achievements.

Finally, we see that this woman "fears the Lord" (v30). Of course she has a strong, personal walk with God. At the same time, surely her husband washes her with the Word (Ephesians 5:26) and treats her with great respect "so that nothing will hinder [his] prayers" (1 Peter 3:7).

■
Exercise 29
HUSBANDS

Answer the following questions:

1. On a scale of 1 to 10, how secure is your wife?

2. Does she worry about the future or can she "laugh at the days to come"?

3. How do you ensure that your children treat her with proper consideration?

4. How do you openly show your appreciation and admiration for her?

5. How do you encourage her successes without fear that she will surpass or outshine you?

6. How do you help her stay strong spiritually and emotionally?

For Wives

Even in the church, anger devastates many marriages. An unwillingness to apologize causes anger to escalate or turn into deep-seated bitterness. In the following passage, Paul instructs wives:

> As the church submits to Christ, so you wives should submit to your husbands in everything. (Ephesians 5:24 NLT)

A decade ago I (Joy) began to reflect on what this verse means when lived out. I decided that, in part, it was telling me to be the first to apologize. It had always seemed unfair—and even dishonest—to apologize when I was 100% sure I was right! How could I say I was sorry for my behavior when I was actually sorry that Adam wouldn't apologize?

I finally realized that there is always something for which I can honestly apologize. Often, it's my prideful, disrespectful attitude. Sometimes it's my competitive heart, or even my unwillingness to trust Adam's leadership (which obviously means I'm not trusting God since he is the one who gave Adam his role in our marriage). I can still struggle with being the first to apologize. Apologizing is always humbling—which I'm sure is exactly where God wants me!

□

Exercise 30
WIVES

Answer the following questions:

1. How do you feel about being the first to apologize?

2. What was your last marital argument about?

3. What were the sins in your behavior or heart?

4. Did you apologize?

5. Were you the first to apologize?

6. If you now realize you could have been more humble, will you go back and discuss this with your husband? If not, why are you unwilling?

7. Are you willing to share these answers with a spiritual friend who can help you grow in this area? (Write down her name!)

Dangerous Territory

Compassion begins with understanding and empathy. Jesus felt compassion for the crowds because he understood their lives— "they were harassed and helpless, like sheep without a shepherd" (Matthew 9:36). When we have a heart for our spouse's struggles and frustrations, being merciful comes more naturally.

Unlike Jesus, we are not able to know each other's thoughts. We have talked with many wives who feel misunderstood by their husbands. They will say, "He doesn't know me, and sometimes I think he doesn't even *want* to know me!" This is a perilous place for spouses. Wives *need* emotional intimacy in the same way that husbands *need* sexual intimacy. When wives don't feel known or understood by their husbands, there is a deep psychological drive for that need to be met, and often the wife finds someone outside the marriage who will meet it.

Seven years into our marriage, I (Joy) felt misunderstood by Adam. I had "tried" to tell him how I felt without much success. I felt unloved and unknown, and I had become hopeless about the future of our relationship. I didn't consciously decide to look for someone else, but at some level I was open to that possibility. I ended up having an extramarital affair. Rather than meeting my emotional need, the affair caused me to feel ashamed and degraded—still unloved and unknown.

So I finally refused to continue seeing the man, and Adam never suspected I had been unfaithful. Seven years later, when I could no longer "live with myself," I confessed my adultery to him.

We both learned much from this period in our lives. First, I (Joy) learned that God will do whatever it takes to humble my out-of-control pride. Of course I am not blaming God, but I have no doubt he allowed me to get deep into sin to help me see that my view of myself as a "righteous person" was off-base! (I was a Sunday School teacher at the time.)

I also learned to recognize the "red flags" in my relationship with Adam. Clearly, when I am not feeling close to Adam—when we are not talking about our relationship, feelings and walk with God—we are in a danger zone. In fact, we have both learned to recognize and point out these warning signs that signal our need for a course correction.

What did I (Adam) learn? To answer that question, I need to give you some history. When I first met Joy she was a legal secretary. I came to her office to do some accounting for her company. Joy was very attractive, and during this assignment I found her to be intelligent, accommodating, pleasant and funny—but more importantly, she made me feel good. I felt she cared about me as a person and respected me. After dating a while we discovered we had a lot in common and enjoyed each other's company. A year and a half later, we were married.

Fast forward fourteen years. One afternoon Joy told me that seven years before she'd had an affair. I was shocked, stunned and speechless. Then I got angry at Joy and the man she'd been with. I couldn't believe something like that would happen *to me.* Joy was very religious, and it dumbfounded me that she could do something like that. I also felt deceived that she hadn't told me for seven years! Again and again, I asked myself how this could happen. To me, everything had seemed fine. I honestly never suspected Joy of anything like that. I felt like a victim.

The more I thought about it, the more I realized Joy had tried to tell me how she was feeling. I should have paid attention when, a decade before, we'd gone to counseling and learned that our needs and expectations were upside down; what was important to me was not important to her, and vice versa.

Then I began to see that I had to take some responsibility for what had happened. Joy was looking for help from me that I didn't give her. I had taken her for granted. In a way, I'd pushed her to do something she'd never normally do. Looking at it that way had a huge impact on me. I thought, "She's the one who has to carry this around for the rest of her life. All it did was put a dent in my ego!" I felt ashamed that I set up the kind of environment that would lead her to do such a thing.

With Joy's help, I learned I was not a very good listener. I was more focused on *fixing* than on understanding. I thought I should have all the answers (and that they were right!). Guess what? I was wrong! I remembered that God gave me Joy as my suitable helper. I should "have full confidence in her because she brings me good, not harm.... She speaks with wisdom, and faithful instruction is on her tongue" (Proverbs 31:11–12, 26). This has made my job as a husband a lot easier and more enjoyable.

* * *

We urge you to learn from our experience! If you do not really know and understand each other—if you are not praying together and discussing your feelings, your hopes and dreams, your plans, and your daily struggles, you are not truly in a "one flesh union." Consider that the King James Version uses the word "know" to indicate sexual union:

Then said Mary unto the angel, How shall this be, seeing I know not a man? (Luke 1:34 KJV)

The New Living Translation tells us that Joseph and Mary were already engaged (Luke 1:27), so although Mary "knew" Joseph (in modern usage), they had not had sexual relations. The bottom line is that if you don't "know" each other emotionally, eventually you may not "know" each other sexually either.

Growing in Compassion

Most of us need a "booster shot" of compassion! How do we begin? By *developing genuine empathy* for each other, learning how to "walk a mile in their shoes."

Self-centeredness prevents us from feeling empathy. We may not have been through exactly what they are experiencing, but we know what it is to feel the same feelings. Talk with your spouse to identify those feelings and then remember a time you felt the same way. (If your "feelings vocabulary" is limited, refer to the feelings chart in the back of the book.)

Remember in as much detail as possible what that feeling was like. What other thoughts or feelings did you have at that time? Discuss what the experience was like for you. This will help you relate to your spouse and recognize what you have in common. Keep in mind that you and your spouse are probably more similar than you are different. You have the same basic desires (attention, recognition, affection and happiness, to name a few). Focus on the similarities instead of the differences.

The next step is *learning to listen* to your spouse "with an intent to understand."[3] Most of us listen with an intent to get our own point across. The next time you are having a discussion, play the role of detective, asking yourself, "What are they really thinking? What are they really feeling?" Paraphrase what you understand: "So it sounds like...." Try reflecting back their feelings: "Sounds like you feel...."

Try to focus on *their* needs, keeping your own concerns at bay. This is a way to encourage your spouse to share more of their inner experience with you, resulting in greater understanding and empathy.

Since being critical is a major impediment to cultivating a spirit of compassion, I (Joy) like to remind myself, "Be compassionate, not critical!" I also committed the following passage to memory:

> So let's stop criticizing each other. Instead, you should decide never to do anything that would make other Christians have doubts or lose their faith. (Romans 14:13 God's Word)

■

Exercise 31
BOTH SPOUSES

Ask each other the following questions:

On a scale of 1–10, how well do I seem to listen and try to understand your feelings?

1. How can I improve my listening skills?

2. Do I communicate that I know what you're feeling?

3. How can I improve?

4. Do you feel *heard and understood* when we communicate?

5. What can I do to improve?

6. Do I seem to struggle with critical thoughts and judgments?

7. Will you point it out to me when I make judgmental comments?

8. Am I quick to forgive (or do I tend to hold grudges)?

9. How can I improve?

Traits of Bible Heroes

Remember that a desire to relieve the suffering of others is the basis of compassion. Now reflect on how each of the following passages illustrates a different Bible hero's compassionate heart:

Joseph: The desire to alleviate fear

> "So then, don't be afraid. I will provide for you and your children." And he reassured them and spoke kindly to them. (Genesis 50:21)

Moses: The desire to alleviate spiritual emptiness

> However, two men, whose names were Eldad and Medad, had remained in the camp. They were listed among the elders, but did not go out to the Tent. Yet the Spirit also rested on them, and they prophesied in the camp. A young man ran and told Moses, "Eldad and Medad are prophesying in the camp." Joshua son of Nun, who had been Moses' aide since youth, spoke up and said, "Moses, my lord, stop them!" But Moses replied, "Are you jealous for my sake? I wish that all the LORD's people were prophets and that the LORD would put his Spirit on them!" (Numbers 11:26–29)

Jonathan: The desire to alleviate loneliness

> [After Saul brought David to be at his palace, taking him away from his father's home] Jonathan took off the robe he was wearing and gave it to David, along with his tunic, and even his sword, his bow and his belt. (1 Samuel 18:4)

Daniel: The desire to alleviate confusion

> Then Daniel answered the king, "You may keep your gifts for yourself and give your rewards to someone else. Nevertheless,

I will read the writing for the king and tell him what it means."
(Daniel 5:17)

Paul: *The desire to prevent eternal suffering*

Do not cause anyone to stumble, whether Jews, Greeks or the
church of God—even as I try to please everybody in every
way. For I am not seeking my own good but the good of
many, so that they may be saved. (1 Corinthians 10:32–33)

Exercise 32
BOTH SPOUSES

Working separately, set aside an hour to reflect on the following questions. Write your answers down, and then share with each other what
you have written.

1. In what ways do I suffer? (Include worries, physical challenges,
   difficult relationships, etc.)

2. In what ways can my spouse help relieve that suffering? (Include prayer, being available to talk, sharing scripture, assisting
   with responsibilities, etc.)

3. In what ways do I see my spouse suffering?

4. In what ways do I believe I can help relieve that suffering?

5. In what ways can we work together to relieve the suffering of
   others in our lives—our children, family members, church
   friends, neighbors or community?

That day on the Mount of Olives, Jesus told his listeners that, if
they would be merciful, God would reward them in kind. Cen-
tral to godliness is a merciful heart:

Who is a God like you,
>   who pardons sin and forgives the transgression
>   of the remnant of his inheritance?
You do not stay angry forever
>   but delight to show mercy.
You will again have compassion on us;
>   you will tread our sins underfoot
>   and hurl all our iniquities into the depths of the sea.
(Micah 7:18–19)

In other words, growing in mercy toward each other enables us to imitate Jesus. This prepares us for the next step—growing in purity of heart (*valuing holiness*), which is the subject of our next chapter.

chapter 9

Value Holiness

"Blessed are the pure in heart,
for they will see God."

Matthew 5:8

As Christians, seeing God one day is our ultimate reward. But Jesus says we must first be pure in heart. In *Discover Joy*, I (Joy) commented that this particular beatitude captures the essence of the gospel:

> If one beatitude expresses the theme of Christ's Sermon on the Mount—in fact, his entire teaching—this is it. Against the backdrop of the Pharisees' legalism, Jesus had come to impart a refreshing message: Your heart is what counts, your inner thoughts and motives are more important to God than the religious rituals you practice or traditions you keep. Most of all, Jesus decried the hypocrisy he saw—those who failed to practice what they preached, those whose worship was about empty routine rather than about genuine faith.[1]

Being pure-hearted means valuing—or *loving*—what is most important to God. But how is this possible for selfish people who are more likely to value what *feels* good rather than what *is* good? Paul's advice is to train our thoughts:

> And now, dear brothers and sisters, one final thing. Fix your thoughts on what is true, and honorable, and right, and pure, and lovely, and admirable. Think about things that are excellent and worthy of praise. (Philippians 4:8 NLT)

Nevertheless, purity can still be challenging. Haven't we all had evil, "crazy" thoughts that pop into our heads? Haven't we all caught ourselves going through the motions of Christianity—reading our Bibles, praying, going to church and even doing "good deeds"—without the heart of *love* that always prompted Jesus?

One reason for this difficulty is that we try to "put the cart before the horse." Remember: The Beatitudes are *progressive steps.* Expecting to be pure and holy without committing to the first five beatitude steps is like expecting a toddler to run a marathon!

On the other hand, when we are consistently humbling ourselves (Matthew 5:3); developing a contrite, repentant heart (Matthew 5:4); surrendering to God and other people (Matthew 5:5); developing a spiritual hunger (Matthew 5:6); and imitating the compassion of Christ (Matthew 5:7), we are ready for this step. Since God is completely holy (Leviticus 19:2), growing more Christlike in all areas of our lives will naturally involve growing to *value holiness.*

What will this mean for your marriage? You will begin to see your spouse as God's amazing gift—chosen just for you. You will be zealous about rooting sin out of your marriage and honoring God with every aspect of your relationship. Finally, you will not only *be* a godly husband or wife, you will *love* doing it!

The Meaning of Purity

Purity encompasses heart (motives), head (thoughts), and hands (behavior). David acknowledged the role of purity in our relationship with God:

> Who may ascend the hill of the LORD?
> Who may stand in his holy place?
> He who has clean hands and a pure heart,
> who does not lift up his soul to an idol
> or swear by what is false. (Psalm 24:3–4)

In the Old Testament, those who were ceremonially unclean could not enter God's house. In the same way, when we are defiled by sin we cannot enjoy fellowship with a holy God. But clean hands are not sufficient without a pure heart. We may wash the outside (by cleaning up our behavior), but God cares if we are clean on the inside—the thoughts and intentions and attitudes of our hearts. Jesus said that the evil that comes out of the heart makes us unclean:

> "For out of the heart come evil thoughts, murder, adultery, sexual immorality, theft, false testimony, slander. These are what make a man 'unclean'; but eating with unwashed hands does not make him 'unclean.'" (Matthew 15:19–20)

Let's begin by looking at what it means to be faithful before considering three different types of infidelity.

How Faithful Are You?

To practice "fidelity" (or be faithful) is to be loyal and trustworthy. This means that when we do anything that is disloyal, untrustworthy or antagonistic to the relationship, we are actually being unfaithful to our spouse.

Notice that infidelity isn't necessarily sexual in nature. The word "unfaithful" applied to our relationship with God infers disloyalty (2 Timothy 2:13)—although at times God does compare it to adultery (Hosea 1:2). The point we're making is that it isn't necessary to commit adultery to be unfaithful.

Loyalty

Have you ever had lustful thoughts about someone who is not your spouse? How about dressing to please or flirting with a co-worker? Have you ever gossiped about your spouse? How about wishing you had a different spouse—maybe someone more sensitive to your needs, or someone with a different personality or a bigger paycheck? These are all acts of disloyalty. On the other hand, to be loyal is to have a single-minded devotion or be completely dependable in our allegiance.

In the Bible, despite being Saul's son, Jonathan chose complete loyalty to David:

> So Jonathan made a pledge of mutual loyalty with David because he loved him as much as {he loved} himself. (1 Samuel 18:3 God's Word)

How was Jonathan able to be so loyal? Because Jonathan loved David as he loved himself! This kind of love can only come from God. No matter how wonderful our spouse is, in our selfish nature we must rely on God for the kind of loyalty that inspires single-hearted devotion.

Since God commands us to honor marriage, any act of disloyalty to our spouse also involves disloyalty to God. It means we are not surrendered to God's plan for our life—that we don't trust God to know what is best for us and to work in our life to transform us into the people he wants us to be. In his letter to the Romans, Paul wrote,

> And we know that God causes everything [even marriage challenges!] to work together for the good of those who love God and are called according to his purpose for them. For

> God knew his people in advance, and he chose them to be-
> come like his Son, so that his Son would be the firstborn
> among many brothers and sisters. (Romans 8:28–29 NLT)

This well-known passage teaches that God has a purpose for each of us that always involves becoming more like Jesus. And since Jesus learned obedience through suffering (Hebrews 5:8), we will also have to experience discomfort and pain. But that suffering is actually for our good, enabling God to bless us even more. (We talked about the value of surrender in Chapter 4, and we encourage you to go back and review that chapter again if necessary.)

Three Types of Infidelity

Deceitfulness

Infidelity begins with deceit. This means misleading your spouse by hiding things and keeping secrets, or not being completely open and truthful. Jesus identified Satan as the father of lies (John 8:44), and throughout the Bible all forms of deception are identified as evil. Reflect on the following passages:

> Deceit is in the heart of those who plan evil,
>   but joy belongs to those who advise peace.
> (Proverbs 12:20 God's Word)

> A malicious man disguises himself with his lips,
>   but in his heart he harbors deceit. (Proverbs 26:24)

> He went on: "What comes out of a man is what makes him
> 'unclean.' For from within, out of men's hearts, come evil
> thoughts, sexual immorality, theft, murder, adultery, greed,
> malice, deceit, lewdness, envy, slander, arrogance and
> folly." (Mark 7:20–22)

> Love is not happy with evil but is happy with the truth.
> (1 Corinthians 13:6 NCV)

■

Exercise 33
BOTH SPOUSES

Working separately, consider and pray through the following questions:

1. When was the last time I intentionally tried to mislead my spouse?

2. What did I do and how does God feel about that?

3. Am I willing to "come clean" with my spouse about my deceit?

4. If not, what am I afraid of?

5. Who can help me in being more truthful with my spouse?

6. What will I do next?

Sexual Impurity

Nowadays, we are concerned about cleaning up the environment. After all, God created this planet and appointed us to rule over it. Pure air and water and food are considered necessities by most people. But not many are so concerned about moral purity.

Because the media—print, movies, television, and so on—has become increasingly more violent, obscene and sexual over the years, many of us have become immune to the dangers of this material. At any time, day or night, we can easily access all types of sexual and pornographic content via our computers, televisions and other forms of electronic media.

Although impurity entails much more than sexuality, we will focus on that area since it has the greatest impact on our marriages.

Since impurity is one of the "deeds of darkness" (Romans 13:12), it is contrary to the life of light to which we are called:

> But among you there must not be even a hint of sexual immorality, or of any kind of impurity, or of greed, because these are improper for God's holy people.... For you were once darkness, but now you are light in the Lord. Live as children of light (for the fruit of the light consists in all goodness, righteousness and truth) and find out what pleases the Lord. (Ephesians 5:3, 8–10)

Impurity involves primarily the mind and heart, although it often leads to behavior such as masturbation (and even adultery). Lustful thoughts usually come from visual stimulation—sexual images we have seen. Jesus talked about the importance of keeping our eyes from evil:

> "The eye is the lamp of the body. If your eyes are good, your whole body will be full of light. But if your eyes are bad, your whole body will be full of darkness. If then the light within you is darkness, how great is that darkness!" (Matthew 6:22–23)

Godly thinking is especially challenging in an era of high technology and loose morality. Although the seductive power of pornography has probably been undermining marriages since the dawn of the printed page, with the easy availability of Internet pornography this practice has become an epidemic.[2]

In her excellent book chronicling her husband's battle with pornography and its devastation on her marriage, Laurie Hall writes,

> The Greek word for "evil"—*poneros*—means "that which is malicious and deliberately harmful of others." In other words, if our eyes are looking at things that are malicious and willfully harming others, we are putting out our own eyes. We are closing ourselves off to truth. The result will

be a plunge into darkness. Relate this to pornography. Whether it's a woman's rape that's carefully recorded and passed around for the "guys" to enjoy, or the defilement of a child that's made available for the appetites of the pedophile, or pictures of the attractive coed who titillates a corporate executive's fantasy, pornography is made by exploiting others for personal gain. Exploiting others for personal gain is evil in its rawest form. A man who feasts his eyes on pictures that have been made by exploiting others is plucking out his own eyes. He is plunging himself into darkness. He will lose his ability to be wise.[3]

Pornography is especially destructive for several reasons: (1) the human brain captures and stores everything we see, "imprinting" the mind by creating a permanent record; (2) these images "pop up" with little provocation or warning; and (3) pornography elicits intense emotional and physical sensations, creating a "rush" like a powerful drug.

Those who experiment with online pornography often move quickly to off-line sexual acting-out. In fact, the late researcher, Dr. Al Cooper, described online sexual behavior as the "crack-cocaine" of compulsive sexuality.

Those who would never consider visiting an online pornographic site need only turn on the television during peak evening hours to experience sexually explicit content.

The fact that few wives can compete with the scantily clad "super-model look" of TV actresses reinforces a worldly perspective and an already shaky sense of self-worth. At the same time, their husbands may struggle with thoughts that they are "settling for second-best."

Exercise 34
HUSBANDS

Answer yes or no to the following questions. Have you_____in the past thirty days?

1. Lingered longer than you should have on a sexually suggestive TV ad or show?

2. Looked at sexual photos?

3. "Checked out" a woman other than your wife?

4. Had lustful fantasies that did not involve your wife?

5. Masturbated?

6. Gone to a pornographic website?

If you answered yes to any of the above, have you talked to your wife about it?

If not, what has prevented you from sharing this with her?

What feelings are you having when you are most vulnerable to temptation in the area of sexual impurity? Anger? Frustration? Discouragement? Loneliness?

Do you have a "godly sorrow" (2 Corinthians 7:10–11) about your sin that involves the following steps: (1) Earnestness/sincerity; (2) Eagerness to clear yourself; (3) Indignation about your sin; (4) Alarm/urgency to change; (5) Longing to be right with God once again; (6) Concern for those you have hurt; and (7) Readiness to see justice done?

Did you speak with a spiritual man who can pray for you, advise you and help you with Scripture?

How do you react when your wife confesses impurity to you? Are you able to listen with understanding and compassion and avoid reacting with anger or self-pity (that might discourage her from being open the next time)?

□
Exercise 35
WIVES

Answer yes or no to the following questions. Have you_____in the past thirty days?

1. Lingered longer than you should have on a sexually suggestive TV ad or show?

2. Looked at sexual photos?

3. "Checked out" a man other than your husband?

4. Had lustful fantasies that did not involve your husband?

5. Masturbated?

6. Gone to a pornographic website?

If you answered yes to any of the above, have you talked to your husband about it?

If not, what has prevented you from sharing this with him?

What feelings are you having when you are most vulnerable to temptation in the area of sexual impurity? Anger? Frustration? Discouragement? Loneliness?

Do you have a "godly sorrow" (2 Corinthians 7:10–11) about your sin that involves the following steps: (1) Earnestness/sincerity; (2) Eagerness to clear yourself; (3) Indignation about your sin; (4) Alarm/urgency to change; (5) Longing to be right with God once again; (6) Concern for those you have hurt; and (7) Readiness to see justice done?

Did you speak with a spiritual woman who can pray for you, advise you and help you with Scripture?

How do you react when your husband confesses impurity to you? Are you able to listen with understanding and compassion and avoid reacting with anger or self-pity (that might discourage him from being open the next time)?

Exercise 36
BOTH SPOUSES

This is your opportunity to discuss your individual answers to the above questions. In order for both of you to feel safe during this exercise, we encourage you to call on another spiritual couple to assist you in having this discussion if either of you thinks it would be helpful or necessary. Remember: You share the same goal—having a more joyful, loving, godly marriage. This is an essential step in that direction!

Instructions for this discussion:

1. Pray together before you begin. Pray specifically that God will give each of you a spirit of patience, kindness and compassion as you have this discussion.

2. Agree that, if at any time either of you feels unsafe, you will end the discussion immediately. (Also agree to get help for your relationship by calling on a spiritual couple or Christian counselor who can advise you and assist with biblical marriage counseling, enabling you to complete this step in the near future.)

3. Discuss your answers to each of the questions. The husband should begin by sharing his responses to the first question. The wife should listen quietly, asking for clarification if necessary. Then proceed to the second question, with the husband sharing his answer. After the husband has answered all the questions, the wife should share with the husband listening quietly, asking for clarification if necessary.

4. Pray together again for wisdom and courage to face any sins or challenges that have come to light

5. Ask for forgiveness, and give forgiveness wherever needed. If you feel unable to forgive, pray for the heart to become more compassionate, and seek spiritual help from a friend.

Adultery

> Honor marriage, and guard the sacredness of sexual intimacy between wife and husband. God draws a firm line against casual and illicit sex. (Hebrews 13:4 Message)

Although we, and many other couples, have learned from personal experience that adultery doesn't have to signal the death of the marriage, marital unfaithfulness is very serious in God's sight. It's also a sign that needs are not being met. That's why couples must frequently ask, "How do you feel about our relationship? Am I meeting your needs?"

In Chapter 5 we recommended that couples have a weekly coffee chat—at least one hour for frank discussion. This is a time set aside to discuss one thing only: *the relationship!* Although it may be more comfortable or natural to discuss work, children or vacation plans, couples must avoid this temptation for the good of the marriage!

Keeping in mind that each of these beatitudes builds on the one before, it's time to take stock of how you're doing as we prepare for the reconciliation skills discussed in the next chapter.

Exercise 37
BOTH SPOUSES
Progress Check

Working separately, complete your own copy of the following Progress Check. Then find an uninterrupted time for discussion. Remember to take responsibility for your own sins and avoid blaming the other (Matthew 7:3–5).

Begin with prayer and then compare your responses, making a plan for working together on the weakest areas.

Answer each of these questions on a 5-point scale, where "1" = poor, "3" = average, and "5" = excellent. If necessary, add a few comments to explain your answer.

Chapter 2

1. How well is your marriage coping with differences in personal style—i.e., compensating for limitations and maximizing opportunities?

2. How is your marriage managing relationships with parents and siblings?

3. Personally, how are you doing in your humility toward your spouse?

Chapter 3

1. How is your marriage doing in progressing toward your joint "Vision Statement" for your relationship?

2. How are you doing in serving your spouse?

3. Personally, how are you doing in minimizing or accepting "little irritations"?

4. How well are you *really listening* to your spouse in an effort to understand?

Chapter 4

1. How are you doing in loving your spouse "as Christ loved the church" (Ephesians 5:25)?

2. How well are you doing in staying close to God so you will be a spiritual mate?

3. How well is each of you "unpacking old baggage" so hurts from the past don't seep in and poison your marriage?

Chapters 5, 6 and 7

1. Personally, how are you doing in being *completely committed* to fulfill God's plan for your marriage?

2. How well is your marriage growing in:

– spiritual unity?

– emotional unity?

– intellectual unity?

– sexual unity?

Chapter 8

1. How are you doing in helping your spouse feel more secure, respected and appreciated?

2. How are you doing in being an example of humility to your spouse?

3. Personally, are you becoming more understanding and quick to forgive?

Chapter 9

1. How are you doing in your willingness to be completely truthful with your spouse?

2. How are you doing in your personal purity?

3. How compassionate are you when your spouse confesses impurity?

Faithful Choices

Considering the modern onslaught of violence, obscenity and pornography in the media, the ability to value holiness by making righteous choices requires us to be clear and passionate about our personal beliefs. Then we must have the courage and self-control to put these beliefs into action. In other words, we must watch both our "life and doctrine" (1 Timothy 4:16).

Fortunately, with Scripture as our guide, we can be crystal clear about the best—in fact, the *only*—way to live. And since "love... comes from a pure heart, a clear conscience, and genuine faith" (1Timothy 1:5 NLT), the more we grow in godliness, the more we will also grow in love! Love, in fact, is the foundation of our next chapter, as we *encourage reconciliation.*

10

Encourage Reconciliation

"Blessed are the peacemakers,
for they will be called sons of God."
Matthew 5:9

In the 1982 Michael Jackson-Paul McCartney hit, "The Girl Is Mine," Michael quips, "Paul, I think I told you I'm a lover, not a fighter."

But it seems most married couples are *both!* In fact, wrestling through conflict and disagreement represents one of those dangerous opportunities that God provides. "Dangerous" because we will not emerge unscathed (Genesis 32:25). An "opportunity" because resolving differences always holds the potential for greater intimacy as we begin to truly understand and connect with each other. The blessing gained in this struggle for oneness with God and each other is the best possible reason to *encourage reconciliation.*

Making War

Even in the church, many couples find that making war is more natural than making peace. Since few of us had parents with effective conflict resolution skills, we must first learn to disagree without falling into the following five destructive patterns.

Harsh criticism – Attacking the spouse's character. Leaves the spouse feeling disliked, blamed, defective or ashamed.

Contempt – Includes behaviors such as name-calling and disgusted facial expressions. It's no surprise that contempt breeds emotional distance and unhappiness, but research actually shows that severe and frequent contempt can be as deadly—physically—as smoking and high cholesterol!

Stonewalling – Icy distance, superiority and distaste. Stonewalling is an attempt at self-protection, intended to "wall" oneself off from emotional pain. It damages the marriage by halting communication, thus preventing the couple from resolving disagreements.

Victimization – One or both spouses see themselves as innocent victims in the marriage. This creates a no-win situation, since a victimized spouse will ignore any attempts at kindness by the other spouse.

Flooding – Spouses are swamped with alarming, out-of-control feelings. They feel increasingly alone and may perceive that divorce is the only reasonable choice.[1]

◨

Exercise 38
BOTH SPOUSES

Are these familiar? Working separately, do the following exercise to decide whether your relationship has fallen prey to the above patterns.

On the right side make a few notes to describe when, what happened, how you felt, and how you resolved (or didn't resolve) the situation:

1. Harsh criticism:

2. Contempt:

3. Stonewalling:

4. Victimization:

5. Flooding:

Now set aside a time with your spouse to review the above exercise. (Include another spiritual couple if this seems wise.) Important: *Avoid blaming your spouse!* Instead, express your own feelings and take responsibility for your actions or reactions: "I think I recognize some of these in our marriage. For example, I feel hurt when you're critical of how the house looks. It seems you think I'm lazy when you say things like, 'I thought you were going to clean today. What have you been doing?' I apologize because now I realize that when I roll my eyes and make sarcastic comments, I'm actually expressing contempt. I know this is disrespectful, and I hope you'll forgive me."

Living together in peace has been a challenge throughout human history. The writers of Proverbs had much to say about quarreling and strife:

> A hot-tempered person starts fights;
>   a cool-tempered person stops them.
> (Proverbs 15:18 NLT)

> Starting a quarrel is like opening a floodgate,
>   so stop before a dispute breaks out.
> (Proverbs 17:14 NLT)

> Anyone who loves to quarrel loves sin;
>   anyone who trusts in high walls invites disaster.
> (Proverbs 17:19 NLT)

> Avoiding a fight is a mark of honor;
>> only fools insist on quarreling. (Proverbs 20:3 NLT)

Of course these words were written before Pentecost. Certainly, living in peace will come more easily with the Holy Spirit living in our hearts. But the fact that Paul and James both addressed quarreling suggests that conflict was common even in the New Testament church. A few examples:

> You are still controlled by your sinful nature. You are jealous of one another and quarrel with each other. Doesn't that prove you are controlled by your sinful nature? (1 Corinthians 3:3 NLT)

> So an elder must be a man whose life is above reproach. He must be faithful to his wife. He must exercise self-control, live wisely, and have a good reputation. He must enjoy having guests in his home, and he must be able to teach. He must not be a heavy drinker or be violent. He must be gentle, not quarrelsome, and not love money. (1 Timothy 3:2–3 NLT)

> What is causing the quarrels and fights among you? Don't they come from the evil desires at war within you? (James 4:1 NLT)

These passages teach that quarreling is unacceptable in the body of Christ. On the other hand, the letters of Paul, Peter and John suggest that God is pleased when we *prevent* conflict by living in a way that eliminates the desire to fight:

> Don't use foul or abusive language. Let everything you say be good and helpful, so that your words will be an encouragement to those who hear them. And do not bring sorrow to God's Holy Spirit by the way you live. Remember, he has identified you as his own, guaranteeing that you will be saved on the day of redemption. Get rid of all bitterness, rage, anger, harsh words, and slander, as well as all types of evil behavior. Instead, be kind to each other, tenderhearted,

forgiving one another, just as God through Christ has forgiven you. (Ephesians 4:29–32 NLT)

Finally, all of you should be of one mind. Sympathize with each other. Love each other as brothers and sisters. Be tenderhearted, and keep a humble attitude. Don't repay evil for evil. Don't retaliate with insults when people insult you. Instead, pay them back with a blessing. That is what God has called you to do, and he will bless you for it. (1 Peter 3:8–9 NLT)

Anyone who loves another brother or sister is living in the light and does not cause others to stumble. But anyone who hates another brother or sister is still living and walking in darkness. Such a person does not know the way to go, having been blinded by the darkness. (1 John 2:10–11 NLT)

Unhealthy Extremes

Most of us do not come into marriage with healthy models of conflict. That was certainly true of our relationship. I (Joy) cannot remember my parents ever disagreeing, but there was certainly tension seething just under the surface. My mother was depressed, while my dad was emotionally shut down.

Adam's family was the other extreme, with frequent yelling and open hostility. With little or no awareness of "fighting fair," arguments would turn ugly, deteriorating into a tirade of personal insults and character assassination.

As a result, we both made early decisions to avoid arguing altogether. Since we'd never even disagree, a casual observer might have been impressed with how well we got along. But we also didn't honestly address our irritations and hurts, so our marriage was like a pressure cooker, and like clockwork, once a year our self-control would "blow," with one huge argument threatening to end the relationship. Afterwards, one of us would usually apologize just to make peace (where there was really no peace). And, since we'd let off some steam—without real reso-lution—typically we'd continue on for another year until our next blow-out would occur.

Eventually, we realized the importance of being more honest with each other on a daily basis; this meant we'd live with the discomfort of sporadic "bumps"—but avoid the annual volcanic eruption!

God's Way to Create and Maintain Unity

The New Testament provides numerous passages that reveal the keys to a harmonious atmosphere. One of our favorites is found in Paul's "rules for holy living" addressed to the Colossian church:

> Therefore, as God's chosen people, holy and dearly loved, clothe yourselves with compassion, kindness, humility, gentleness and patience. Bear with each other and forgive whatever grievances you may have against one another. Forgive as the Lord forgave you. And over all these virtues put on love, which binds them all together in perfect unity. (Colossians 3:12–13)

Many couples seem to think that, although this sounds good, it just isn't realistic or possible. But notice how Paul begins. He sets the stage, reminding us that we are "God's chosen people, holy and dearly loved...." Only with God's Spirit are we able to overcome our selfishness. Paul knew that a *godly self-image*—our ability to view ourselves as God does—is a powerful motivator to live in a way that glorifies him and brings us great satisfaction and joy.

Remember the twelve scouts sent out by Moses to explore Canaan? Ten of them reported, "We can't attack those people; they are stronger than we are.... We seemed like grasshoppers in our own eyes, and we looked the same to them" (Numbers

13:31, 33). However, Joshua and Caleb didn't see themselves as grasshoppers; they saw themselves as God did, so they were God-confident and full of faith, sure of his power and promises.

Next, Paul tells us to "clothe" ourselves with compassion, kindness, humility, gentleness and patience. We are to allow God to transform us by putting these attributes on and wearing them, much in the same way that a beautiful dress or handsome suit can transform the way we look, feel and act. Does God really want us to put on an "act," pretending to be something that we really don't feel inside?

There is no doubt that God cares about the heart. At the same time, psychologists know that change occurs in both directions: Just as attitude change will eventually result in changed behavior, changing our actions will also lead us to change our intentions, beliefs, perceptions and attitudes. This happens because people are trying to be consistent in their attitudes and behaviors.

The next sentence tells us to "bear with" each other and forgive any grievances we hold against the other. In the New Living Translation, this reads, "Make allowance for each other's faults, and forgive anyone who offends you." As discussed in previous chapters, this is much easier when we remember our own shortcomings.

Finally, we are to "put on love," which Paul observes, "binds them all together in perfect unity." Love is the glue that keeps us together. I (Adam) have learned to use the characteristics of love listed in 1 Corinthians 13:4–7 as a personal barometer to determine how I'm doing as a husband. When Joy and I aren't unified or she is feeling insecure or unhappy in our relationship, I ask myself, "Am I being patient? Kind? Am I envious or boastful or proud? Am I being rude or self-seeking? Am I easily angered? Am I holding on to grudges? Am I eager for the truth to come out? Am I protecting and trusting Joy? Am I hopeful? Am I persevering?" Inevitably, somewhere in that passage I'll identify the ways I need to change.

Conflict, God's Way

Before we discuss biblical direction for turning conflict into an opportunity for greater understanding and intimacy, let's discuss one of the most common ways conflict begins.

The basis of Dr. Emerson Eggerichs' excellent book, *Love and Respect,* is a pattern he calls "the Crazy Cycle." We have observed this phenomenon in many marriages (including our own), and firmly believe it is the number one source of destructive fighting. Eggerichs says,

> When a husband feels disrespected, he has a natural tendency to react in ways that feel unloving to his wife. (Perhaps the command to love was given to him precisely for this reason!) When a wife feels unloved, she has a natural tendency to react in ways that feel disrespectful to her husband. (Perhaps the command to respect was given to her for this reason!)
>
> The Love and Respect Connection is clearly within Scripture, but so is the constant threat that the connection can be strained or even broken. And then came what I call the "aha" moment: this thing triggers itself. Without love, she reacts without respect. Without respect, he reacts without love—ad nauseam. Thus was born the Crazy Cycle![2]

To discover whether this pattern is true of your marriage, complete the following exercise in preparation for our next section.

Exercise 39
BOTH SPOUSES

Answer the following questions, and then share your answers with your spouse:

1. What are some things your spouse does that feel unloving? What would you like them to do differently in these areas? (Be specific!)

2. What are some things your spouse does that feel disrespectful? What would you like them to do differently in these areas? (Be specific!)

Top Ten Tips for Reconciliation

Have the Courage to Confront
Those of us who fear rejection prefer to avoid disagreements. But healthy intimate relationships require honesty. The first step is to remember that your security comes from God (see Exodus 14:14 and Psalm 16:5–8). Next, if your natural tendency is to avoid conflict due to fear, remember that confronting your spouse is actually an act of love.

Not only is it unhealthy to "stuff" feelings rather than open up and work toward resolution, the things that are *not said* often cause more trouble in relationships than the things that *are said.* Finally, 1 John 1:7 teaches that enjoying fellowship with each other only comes from walking in the light, so couples who keep things out in the open are able to achieve a greater level of intimacy.

Discuss Concerns As Soon As Possible
Ephesians 4:26 tells us not to let the sun go down while we are

still angry. This is great advice for married couples. Deal with issues quickly so you don't end up harboring resentment, bitterness and grudges. Irritations are like little splinters that can fester and eventually get infected. Deal with them quickly—before gangrene sets in and an amputation is necessary!

Pray for Humility Before You Talk

It's normal to feel that *you are right* (which means your spouse is wrong!). This is why it's so important to pray first. Ask God for the ability to be "completely humble and gentle" (Ephesians 4:2), and for the willingness to really hear and understand your spouse's viewpoint. Also pray for a non-defensive attitude, a readiness to admit how you reacted badly or hurt your spouse. Remember that since none of us has "arrived," we all need help to grow, and God has given each of us a personal "growth coach" (our spouse).

Say It with Care and Clarity

Your goal is to build a "best friendship" with your spouse, so talk to them with the same care you would use in addressing a best friend (Ephesians 4:29). Express your own feelings in a clear and direct way, making sure your spouse understands. At the same time, be concise. Don't beat around the bush or be long-winded. The goal is not to beat your spouse up with your words, but simply to communicate your needs and feelings in a way that increases the likelihood that your spouse will hear them and respond in a constructive way. Fights usually begin, not because of *what* is said, but *how* it is said.

Be Truthful and Loving

In Ephesians 4:15, Paul writes that "speaking the truth in love" helps us grow up spiritually, becoming more like Christ. Think about Jesus' interaction with the Samaritan woman (John 4:4–42). Without harshness or condemnation, he confronted the woman about her sinful lifestyle. Always patient and compassionate, Jesus didn't hesitate to tell the truth, pointing out the need for personal change. This skill is essential in healthy relationships, but it is not necessarily easy. Speaking the truth requires the courage to risk confrontation regardless of the consequences—loving the truth more than approval or agreement.

On the other hand, being loving requires gentleness—caring deeply and unconditionally about people regardless of their weaknesses or sins. We must learn to engage in both of these behaviors at the same time. Unfortunately, many of us are comfortable with one or the other: confrontation without much compassion or compassion without much confrontation!

How can we find the balance between these two extremes? When I (Joy) worked in leadership development, I came up with a strategy to help managers overcome the tendency to present all correction in a negative way. I called it "Constructive Correction." Although my training sessions were typically intended for business managers, the basic principles are the same in any interpersonal relationship.

Here's how it works: Before you tell your spouse about something that bothers you, express gratitude for something you appreciate. Many of us take positive behavior for granted, rarely expressing appreciation but quickly letting kids or spouse know when their behavior needs to change.

Here's an example of Constructive Correction: "Honey, I really appreciate your making the bed on the days I have to leave for work early. I feel irritated, though, when you leave all your unwashed breakfast dishes in the sink for me to do when I get home. Would you be willing to rinse them and put them in the dishwasher before you leave?" Beginning with a positive increases the likelihood that your spouse will be willing to hear your request without defensiveness. (This is not manipulation as long as your expressions of appreciation are given sincerely and frequently—not just when you want your spouse's cooperation.)

According to Willard Harley, author of *Love Busters: Overcoming Habits that Destroy Romantic Love,* each of us has a "Love Bank."[3] Harley says that "when someone does something that makes us feel good, love units are deposited into their account. And when he or she does something that makes us feel bad, love units are withdrawn." Critical, selfish demands are common in marriages with a negative "bank balance," and when negatives outweigh positives, the relationship is in trouble. Expressions of appreciation go a long way to ensure that your Love Bank has a healthy balance!

Learn by Listening

Jesus taught that our mouths express the things that are in our hearts (Matthew 12:34.) This means that listening is one of the best ways to get to know each other. If someone asked you to describe your spouse's values, hopes, dreams, fears and worries, could you do this? Couples often say they need help with their communication, but then they admit they tend to live their hectic lives without ever really listening to each other.

As a clinical psychologist, one of my (Joy's) major tasks involves simply listening and then communicating to my clients that they have been heard and understood. Notice that while listening is the first step, it's also important to respond in a way that lets the other person know you have in fact heard and understood them.

Although listening is a skill most of us can learn, *intention* is the first step. In order to step outside our selfish concerns and distractions, our desire to understand must be greater than our desire to get our own needs met. Do you really want to know and understand your spouse? If so, practice listening with an intent to understand, and then paraphrase their message to see if you really got it: "You're saying that..." or "Sounds like you think ..." If feelings were expressed, say, "You sound [angry, frustrated, irritated, etc.] because..." Responding this way will communicate that you care enough to listen and also encourage your spouse to view you as a trusted confidante.

Don't Dredge Up Old Wounds

Those of us who spent years stuffing our feelings can use disagreements as an opportunity to "dump" all that leftover emotion. Rather than focusing on the issue that prompted the discussion, we may veer off into old hurts. When we do that, I (Adam) try to stop for a moment and say, "But that's yesterday's newspaper." This alerts both of us that we're getting off the topic at hand. Paul teaches in 1 Corinthians 13:5 that love "keeps no record of wrongs." This means we must work to imitate God, who has "removed our sins as far from us as the east is from the west" (Psalm 103:12 NLT).

Beware of Black-and-White Thinking

"You're always complaining about my cooking!" Phil fumed to Paula's comment that the chicken seemed a little dry. Paula responded with, "That's not fair! I never complain about your cooking!"

Do you use words like "always," "never," "right," "wrong," "good" and "bad" in your conversations? If so, you may view events or people in all-or-nothing terms. In psychology, this is known as a "cognitive distortion" because reality is rarely that clear-cut.

How is black-and-white thinking a problem? People who think in black-and-white terms often learned that they—and everything in life—must be perfect, so they become anxious and depressed when they're unable to live up to that standard. They also have difficulty feeling grateful because nothing is ever quite good enough. They often make statements like, "If only..., things would be perfect." Trapped in their own imperfection, they may try to escape through workaholism, drug abuse or even suicide.

What does black-and-white thinking do to marriages? The spouse who thinks in black-and-white terms will find it difficult to accept and appreciate his or her mate, always focusing on the things that are *not* right. When both spouses are black-and-white thinkers, arguments can quickly turn into "World War III" as they defend themselves and lash out at each other.

If black-and-white thinking is damaging your relationship, here are a few suggestions:

- Recognize that positive (faithful) thinking has a biblical basis. Paul told the Philippians,

  > Whatever is true, whatever is noble, whatever is right, whatever is pure, whatever is lovely, whatever is admirable—if anything is excellent or praiseworthy—think about such things. (Philippians 4:8)

- Agree to help each other by pointing out instances of black-and-white or negative thinking.

- Help the black-and-white spouse to recognize the various ways he or she discounts positive experiences, and the detrimental effect this is having. Other types of negative thinking include *fortune telling,* which involves making negative predictions, ("I'll never get that job."); *labeling* ("He's such a loser." or "She's just lazy."); *overgeneralizing* ("I accidentally erased that file. I can't do anything right." or "I spent one whole hour in line to get my car license. Life stinks!"); *heart talk,* in which you treat feelings as reality, ("I feel like a failure; therefore I am a failure); and *shoulda-musta-oughta* ("I keep beating myself up because I should have known not to do that.")

- Take advantage of the abundance of available resources for overcoming negative thinking (also called ANTS—"automatic negative thoughts"). A good place to begin is online. One simple technique is called "thought stopping": Google "thought stopping instructions" for more information. Another great resource is Tom Jones's book *Mind Change.*[4]

Avoid Personal Insults

Keep in mind that your foremost goal, even in disagreements, is always greater understanding and unity. That's why starting a grievance with the word "you" is rarely a good idea. Statements beginning with "you" often come across as accusations. Instead, take responsibility for your own feelings. Rather than, "You are unloving," say, "I feel unloved" or "That felt unloving." Focus on the issue, not your spouse's character.

In the previous section, we mentioned that "labeling" is an example of negative thinking. Now we will go one step further and say it's a form of destructive communication. When labeling reflects an underlying heart that needs to change, this can be addressed later—as part of a gentle, loving discussion—not in the context of a disagreement. In other words, discuss the specific issues that led to the disagreement first. Once these have been resolved, the "heart" issues can be addressed (either immediately or later at an appropriate time).

Being Unified Is More Important Than Being Right!

In the final analysis, remember that marital conflict is not a win-lose situation. The resolution should benefit both spouses and bring your relationship into greater harmony. It should re-establish your emotional bond and heal your relationship, fulfilling the promise that this "obstacle" was in fact an *opportunity* for growth and intimacy.

◼

Exercise 40
BOTH SPOUSES

Answer the following questions, then take some time to discuss your answers with your spouse:

1. Which of the above tips do you want to put into practice?

2. As you think through the tips, in what ways do you realize you can repent and grow personally?

3. In what ways can your spouse grow?

4. On a scale of 1 to 10, how faithful are you that the two of you can work together to transform your conflict from an obstacle into an opportunity for greater understanding and unity? If you are not optimistic about this, who will you call on for help?

How wonderful, how beautiful,
    when brothers and sisters get along!
(Psalm 133:1 Message)

We began this workbook by saying that God wants us to delight in our spouse. How can we achieve this delight? By finding great unity in our marriages, which brings us great fulfillment and joy while also helping us to glorify God. The fact is that truly unified marriages are so unusual they can inspire those around us. Our next chapter, "Reflect the Heart of Christ," provides a vision for using your delightful, inspiring marriage to change the world.

chapter

11

Reflect the Heart of Christ

"Blessed are those who are persecuted because of righteousness,
for theirs is the kingdom of heaven."

Matthew 5:10

Discover Joy showed how living Jesus' Beatitudes results in vibrant mental health, joy and spiritual fruit regardless of our outward circumstances. In Chapter 9, I (Joy) wrote,

> The more we know Christ and share his heart—his character, motives, passions—the more willing and eager we will be to...give up anything or suffer in any way to advance his kingdom. And because we have his power, the more we will be able to perform "miracles" (although actually it will be Christ living in us).[1]

The underlying message of this current book is that the Beatitudes are more than a guide for *personal* spiritual growth; in fact, God works his miracles in the marriage relationship (and all our relationships) when we live the Beatitudes on a daily basis. We could call Matthew 5:3–10 "God's perfect blueprint" for a *delightful marriage,* a relationship that brings great delight to him—and to us!

Now, with gratitude for his amazing work in our lives, it's time to offer our marriages back to God as "living sacrifices" (Romans 12:1). Just as Priscilla and Aquila glorified God in their relationship, God wants our marriages to shine like stars in a dark world as we *reflect the heart of Christ.*

Jesus' Greatest Desire

What did Jesus want more than anything? In short, he wanted God's will to be done, to glorify God by completing the work God had given him to do on earth (John 17:4). That work involved preaching the Good News of the Kingdom (Luke 4:43), seeking and saving the lost (Luke 19:10), and giving his life as a ransom for many (Matthew 20:28).

Basically, Jesus wanted everyone to know the joy and blessing that could be theirs if they simply trusted and followed his Father's way (John 10:10). His priority was spreading the Word, what we now call "evangelism."

Jesus' absolute commitment to God's will is demonstrated by his willingness to pay an immeasurable price to see his will be done. The sacrifices he made are difficult for most of us to fathom. Jesus gave up *everything:* home (Matthew 8:20), family acceptance (Mark 3:21), popularity (Mark 6:2–3), food and rest (Mark 6:31), safety (Luke 13:31–32), friendship (Mark 14:50), justice (Acts 8:33) and ultimately his life!

While it is unlikely that we will be called to make all these sacrifices, how can we begin to reflect Jesus' heart by ensuring that our marriages are ready to be used by God?

Invite Jesus to 'Master' Your Relationship

The first step in making your marriage effective for evangelism is making sure Jesus is Lord of your relationship and your life (1 Peter 3:15-16). When we were baptized we declared, "Jesus is Lord!" But as "life happens," we may forget (or forsake) our vows to God. So we must continually test ourselves to assess our faith and commitment (2 Corinthians 13:5).

Working separately, reflect on the following questions. Then come together for discussion, sharing your responses and giving each other encouragement and spiritual help.

■

Exercise 41
HUSBANDS

1. Is Jesus still Lord of my life? What is the evidence that this is/is not true?

2. Does our marriage honor and please him?

3. Are there areas of our marriage that are not godly?

4. Am I one hundred percent committed to obey the *entire* Bible— even the more "difficult" teachings about marriage such as Ephesians 5:22 (wives) and Ephesians 5:28 (husbands)?

5. If Jesus were coming to dinner, would we try to pretend that our marriage or family is different than it really is?

6. Am I willing to risk the possible humiliation of complete transparency—telling the whole truth about our relationship so we can get the help we need?

Your answers to these questions will reveal the areas where you still need prayer, repentance and spiritual guidance.

This doesn't mean your marriage has to be perfect before you can use it for God's glory! One of the best ways to inspire non-Christian couples is to talk about how God has already worked to change your relationship, and how you realize it is still "a work in progress" as you continue to practice biblical principles and seek spiritual help for certain areas of your marriage. After forty-five years of marriage (and more than fifteen years as baptized disciples), we are still excited to see what God will teach us next!

The passage that best explains how to *reflect the heart of Christ* is found just a few verses after the Beatitudes:

> "If I make you light-bearers, you don't think I'm going to hide you under a bucket, do you? I'm putting you on a light stand. Now that I've put you there on a hilltop, on a light stand— shine! Keep open house; be generous with your lives. By opening up to others, you'll prompt people to open up with God, this generous Father in heaven." (Matthew 5:15–16 Message)

Be Creative

The question is, how can God use the things you're learning to inspire other couples to seek a relationship with him? Look for opportunities to show others what God is doing in your life! A few examples are as follows:

- Invite your neighbors to a small group Bible discussion where the topic is "Rekindling the Excitement in Your Marriage."

- Make the most of opportunities to be vulnerable, sharing the marriage challenges you have faced and the ways God is transforming your relationship.

- Invite non-Christian couples to marriage retreats and workshops sponsored by your church (and then encourage them to study the Bible afterward).

- When friends share their marriage struggles, invite them into your home for a time of fellowship and Bible study.

- Reach out to neighbors by being hospitable whenever possible. Invite other couples for dinner or to spend Sunday afternoon watching the game (and munching on finger foods). Include another couple from church who can help steer the discussion toward spiritual topics.

- Work with another couple to host a game night for five to ten couples, including non-Christian friends. Ask people to bring an appetizer, and set up several tables so everyone can choose their favorite games (cards, dominoes, charades, etc.)

Exercise 42
BOTH SPOUSES

Working separately, answer the following questions. Then come together to discuss your answers.

1. Rate the degree to which your marriage shines light in a dark world:

   1   2   3   4   5   6   7   8   9   10
   Not at all   Somewhat   Completely

2. Explain your answer.

3. What are the obstacles that have prevented you from being more evangelistic? (Examples: overwhelmed by our own problems, not believing God will use us, discouragement, complacency, etc.)

4. In what specific ways are you currently working together to reach the non-Christian community? (Examples: hospitality, inviting couples to church, hosting evangelistic small group Bible studies, etc.)

5. What additional ideas do you have for helping your friends become Christians?

In his book *Lifestyle Evangelism,* Joe Aldridge writes,

> Many budding fishers of men are defeated before they get a line in the water because they are convinced no one is interested, seeking, or prepared by God. Our Lord has already told us the fields are ripe for harvest. Believe me there are Spirit-prepared people living near you who are seeking answers.... For many, the first step in neighborhood evangelism is attitudinal. If they think they will be successful or unsuccessful, they will. What we anticipate in life is usually what we get. If you believe you can't do it, you're probably right. But God says you can. Who do you intend to believe?[2]

This being said, we admit that if there is one main area of our marriage where we need to grow, it is in evangelism. We enjoy entertaining couples, including those who are not yet Christians, but we must work on turning an enjoyable evening into a desire to know more about God and his word.

Be Prepared

Matthew 5:10 talks of being persecuted for righteousness, so it is inevitable that "reflecting the heart of Christ" will eventually get us in trouble. In fact, the more we are living the kingdom life, the more likely it is that someone will be offended. Jesus said,

> "Do you remember what I told you? 'A slave is not greater than the master.' Since they persecuted me, naturally they will persecute you. And if they had listened to me, they would listen to you." (John 15:20 NLT)

Persecution can take many forms. If you live in the United States, it will most likely be relatively subtle, such as the colleagues who choose not to invite you to their holiday party (because you "probably wouldn't enjoy it anyway"). Although this kind of persecution may be "minor," it can still hurt, especially when your children suffer. If your neighbor fails to include preteen Lizzie in her daughter's surprise birthday party (because you "might not approve" of the games the girls will play), your daughter might resent your faith since she hasn't yet come to personally know the ways God blesses his committed children. (Prayerfully, she will also remember your commitment and be inspired by your passion for the gospel!)

Any discussion of persecution must note that there are Christians even today who live in daily fear of being jailed or executed for their faith. Intending no disrespect, perhaps we should call the experience of U.S. Christians "discrimination" to avoid even suggesting that what we are going through can begin to compare to their sufferings.

The question is not whether true persecution involves incarceration or torture, but whether we are willing to obey and follow Christ—*wherever* he leads. This is the heart God is seeking—fully committed and surrendered to his will.

▚

Exercise 43
BOTH SPOUSES

Answer the following questions, and then share your answers with each other:

1. What price are you willing to pay to allow God to use your marriage for his purposes?

2. Are you allowing fear to hold you back?

3. Can you honestly say you "reflect the heart of Christ" in your

desire to follow him, regardless of the sacrifice? If not, are you willing to work toward repentance in this area?

4. Specifically, what will your repentance look like and what will you do differently?

Be Passionate

Robert Coleman concludes his classic little book, *The Master Plan of Evangelism,* with the following statement:

> When will we realize that evangelism is not done by something, but by someone? It is an expression of God's love... now expressed through his Spirit in the lives of those yielded to him.... This is the new evangelism we need. It is not better methods, but better men and women who know their Redeemer from personal experience—men and women who see his vision and feel his passion for the world—men and women who are willing to be nothing so that he might be everything—men and women who want only for Christ to produce his life in and through them according to his own good pleasure.[3]

Are you as inspired by this quote as we are? Join us in devoting yourselves to this vision with all the energy and passion Christ gives you. Then, together, may we delight in his love and in each other, and *reflect the heart of Christ!*

With much prayer that you will *Discover Joy in Your Marriage,*

Adam & Joy Bodzioch

Feelings Chart

GLAD	MAD	SAD	SCARED
At ease	Bothered	Down	Uneasy
Secure	Irritated	Blue	Cautious
Comfortable	Annoyed	Low	Tense
Contented	Steamed	Disappointed	Anxious
Optimistic	Perturbed	Downhearted	Distressed
Satisfied	Fed Up	Unhappy	Frightened
Pleased	Disgusted	Mournful	Agitated
Encouraged	Indignant	Grieved	Alarmed
Tickled	Ticked Off	Depressed	Overwhelmed
Thrilled	Fuming	Crushed	Frantic
Delighted	Irate	Defeated	Panic Stricken
Joyful	Incensed	Wretched	Petrified
Exhilarated	Outraged	Despairing	Terrified
Ecstatic	Furious	Devastated	Numb

CONFUSED	LONELY	ASHAMED
Uncertain	Awkward	Out of Place
Unsettled	Disconnected	Self-Conscious
Perplexed	Invisible	Embarrassed
Flustered	Unwelcome	Flustered
Unfocused	Excluded	Sorry
Fragmented	Insignificant	Remorseful
Dismayed	Ignored	Guilty
Insecure	Neglected	Belittled
Bewildered	Detached	Humiliated
Stunned	Unwanted	Violated
Chaotic	Rejected	Dirty
Torn	Abandoned	Mortified
Baffled	Desolate	Defiled
Dumbfounded	Forsaken	Degraded

NOTES

Introduction

1. J. Bodzioch, *Discover Joy* (Spring Hill, TN: DPI, 2009).

Chapter 1: As Christ Loved the Church

1. S.D. and M.K. Gordon, "Quiet Talks on Home Ideals," *Bible Explorer* (WORDsearch Corp., 2009).
2. H.D. Thoreau, *Walden,* 1854.
3. *Christian Post E-Newsletter*:
http://www.christianpost.com/services/newsletter/daily/
4. R. Beavers and R.B. Hampson, "The Beavers Systems Approach to Family Assessment," *Journal of Family Therapy* 22 Vol. 2 (2000), 128–143. (Available from: onlinelibrary.wiley.com)

Chapter 2: Decide to Trust God's Way

1. From Matthew Henry's *Unabridged Commentary* online.

Chapter 4: Surrender to Each Other

1. Wives who choose to remain faithful to their non-Christian husbands still bear a primary responsibility to protect their children. If a husband becomes abusive, the wife must take steps to ensure that her children are shielded from this abuse. This may involve asking the spouse to move out of the home for a time. Clearly, she should seek input from elders or other mature Christians about godly decisions in these situations.
2. J. Bodzioch, "Benefits of Suffering," *Discover Joy* (Spring Hill, TN: DPI, 2009), 39.
3. L. Dillow, *Calm My Anxious Heart* (Colorado Springs, CO: Navpress, 1998), 154.
4. J. Piper, www.soundofgrace.com/piper89/6-11-89.htm
5. Ibid.
6. J. Gottman, *Why Marriages Succeed or Fail: And How You Can Make Yours Last* (New York: Fireside/Simon & Schuster, 1994), 18.
7. Gottman, 61.

Chapter 5: Commit to Grow in Faith and Love: Part 1

1. E. Wheat and G.O. Perkins, *Love Life for Every Married Couple* (Grand Rapids: Zondervan, 1980), 27.

2. B. Cannon, News Release: http://www.virginia.edu/uvatoday/newsRelease.php?print=1&id=12551

Chapter 7: Commit to Grow in Faith and Love: Part 3

1. J. Gray, *Men Are from Mars, Women are from Venus* (New York: Harper Collins, 1992).

2. D. Tannen, *You Just Don't Understand* (New York: Ballentine/Harper Collins, 1990).

3. From Stanford School of Medicine: Women's Health. Online: http://womenshealth.stanford.edu/fsm/sensate_focus.html

Chapter 8: Overflow with Compassion

1. E.W. Goodrick and J.R. Kohlenberger, *The NIV Exhaustive Concordance, 2nd Edition* (Grand Rapids, MI: Zondervan, 1999).

2. R.C. Roberts, *Taking the Word to Heart* (Grand Rapids, MI: Eerdmans, 1993).

3. S. Covey, *The Seven Habits of Highly Effective People* (New York: Free Press/Simon & Schuster, 2004), 240.

Chapter 9: Value Holiness

1. J. Bodzioch, *Discover Joy* (Spring Hill, TN: DPI, 2009), 121.

2. Recent statistics show that 25% of total search engine requests and 8% of total emails are porn-related. Average daily pornographic emails are 4.5 per Internet user, and 12% of total websites are pornographic. Sexhelp.com, a website offering assistance to people suffering from sexual addiction, reports that over 70% of sex addicts report having problematic online sexual behavior and two-thirds of those thus engaged have such despair over their Internet activities that they have had suicidal thoughts.

3. L. Hall, *An Affair of the Mind* (Colorado Springs, CO: Focus on the Family, 1996), 68.

Chapter 10: Encourage Reconciliation

1. J. Gottman, *What Predicts Divorce* (New York: Taylor & Francis, 1993), 134–140.

2. E. Eggerichs, *Love & Respect* (Colorado Springs, CO: Focus on the Family, 2004), 16.

3. W. Harley, *Love Busters* (Grand Rapids, MI: Revell/Baker, 2004), 21.

4. T. Jones, *Mind Change* (Spring Hill, TN: DPI, 1996, 2007).

Chapter 11: Reflect the Heart of Christ

1. J. Bodzioch, *Discover Joy*, 172.

2. J. Aldrich, *Lifestyle Evangelism* (Colorado Springs, CO: Waterbrook Multnomah Publishing, 1993), 175–176.

3. R. Coleman, *The Master Plan of Evangelism* (Grand Rapids, MI: Baker, 1993), 105–106.